Dare to be a Badass!

Find Your Voice, Find Your Power,

Find Your Purpose!

© 2021
By Pamala J Vincent

Why I wrote this book:

As a teenager, I was blessed to have excellent mentors in my life. They taught me things as simple as French braiding my hair to canning for providing quality, inexpensive food for my family. I had women share how to build my confidence, how to look for a forever partner, my best power colors, and how to find my personal purpose.

Family health challenges, 2020's Covid-19, and evacuating from wildfires in our hometown made me re-evaluate what is important. I am healthy, but what if I should die, like many others before me, what tribal knowledge would pass with me? With you? I am compelled to speak what others have taught along-side the lessons from the university of hard knocks. What message might we leave behind to those who are engaged in the battle for abundance in life?

I meet so many women who wander aimlessly looking to fill a gap in their lives that cannot be filled from the outside. The joy and abundance of life comes from a place inside each of us. It's a place that is confident, responsive (rather than reactive), that dares to dream big dreams and able to make a mark in the world that leaves us all better for the future. I want to be a part of that change in an individual.

I'm not famous. I'm not the smartest person you will meet, but I am observant and willing to pass on what I've learned. I believe by equipping ourselves, we build warriors, a strong family, a community, and a powerful nation.

Defining yourself is an essential step to moving forward toward your purpose in life. Once you have asked and answered the questions that describe you, you will be much better equipped to make choices regarding your path in life.

I pray great blessings for you as you walk this discovery and define your purpose. Your gifting is within you and is given for the sake of others. Discovering you and your strengths will enrich and bless your life and all you meet around you. Don't wait to be a blessing to you and your circle of influence.

Mahalo.

Dedication

It is always difficult to thank the people who inspire a book. There are so many who support my writing that I would be crushed if I forgot one. From the concept to the editing, I have been blessed with a myriad of family and friends who have watched this project from idea to the last page. I pray you know who you are and I thank you all.

Your never-failing encouragement inspired me to continue to put words on paper in an order that I pray touches a heart string which propels you to be the Badass warriors you already are and are becoming.

This book is by you and for you all,

Pamala J Vincent

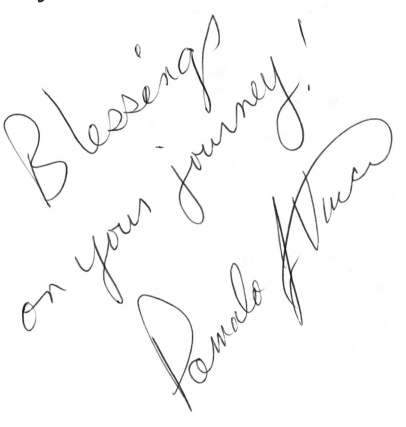

Table of Contents

Introduction:

Women are unique warriors created to care for families, businesses, communities, and nations. We often become battle-weary when we don't define our strengths. We may find ourselves powerless, voiceless, and purposeless.

Like the warrior who pulled the sword from the stone, the power to influence for greatness lies within you. When we discover our purpose, we uncover the gold our creator meant to shine when He us knit together.

It's time to pick up our swords and take back the battlefields.

Dare to be a Badass, created to sharpen weapons of a woman's daily war, equips and challenges women to take their rightful place in their circles of influence. Each chapter discusses a daily life issue, gives 3-5 practical life-hacks and five Pick Up Your Sword work pages.

We face battles on a wide variety of fronts and knowing who we are created to be defines which battles to engage for success in our homes, work, and spiritual lives.

This book is for women who dare to make a difference. We need to glean the wisdom of the women who have come before us and be the voice for the next generation.

Offer yourself as a role model of good actions.

Show integrity, seriousness, and a sound message that is above criticism when you teach, so that any opponent will be ashamed because they won't find anything bad to say about us.

~ Titus 2:7-8

Louisa May Alcott (1832-1888).

https://www.biography.com/people/louisa-may-alcott-9179520
Alcott worked to support her family through financial difficulties at an early age, and managed to write "Little Women," one of the most famous novels in American history. Her other famous writings include "Little Men" and "Jo's Boys."

Lesson 1

What is a Badass?

"One does not discover new lands
without consenting to lose sight of the shore."
~Andre Gide

The term Badass might conjure up a leather wearing, motorcycle riding, tattoo covered, beer swigging woman, up to no good. In other parts of the world, the term Badass means a woman who is in charge of her life. She has moved from talking about doing to actually doing. She knows she needs to change and is taking the steps to make those changes happen.

Badassness is more about discovering who we are, our unique strengths and finding our purpose. Our calling or best self might be to raise a family, to create a business that supports other households, to find a cure for cancer, to care for a neighbor, rescue animals or teach a child to read. However, to do our best work, we need to know our strengths, skills, and gifting. Understanding our personality type, how we learn, how we show we care, and our personal mission will guide us to develop our best self.

Our brains are wired to protect us and keep us from danger. Unfortunately, staying 'safe' can also keep us stuck. Too often we go to work, pay bills, to work so we can pay bills. Somewhere along the details of life we stop dreaming and just settle for mediocre lives.

There comes a day when staying stuck is more painful than bravely moving forward and wanting more.

A Badass woman takes inventory of her life, takes steps to define who she is, confronts the obstacles that hold her back, and sets about building a forward strategy. Then she takes the first step. And then the next. We won't become all we are designed to be over night; it's a process, but we do need to take a step forward, get out of our way, and then take the next step forward.

Warning! When we start to make changes, some people in our circle of influence may resist those efforts. Knowing who we are, where we are going and why, will make the journey doable and bearable. As difficult as it is to hear, our loved ones may be the biggest obstacles to changing our life. Do it anyway!

They'll figure it out as they watch us succeed and perhaps join us or offer support. They may criticize our plans and may have advice for us. Do not be offended.

Their personal rules and doing the same thing daily may give them a false sense of security. Veering away from their methods may frighten them or they may just be concerned for us. They may also be envious of our bravery and their lack of such. People get comfortable with who we are with both our role and theirs. When we begin to change the roles, we force them to re-access theirs—something they may not be ready for. Remember, our success is not always a straight line and is not dependent on whether other people accept what we recognize is our purpose. We serve an audience of one and we only answer to Him.

Warrior women understand they are created for more than a dreary life. Scripture promises us that we were built for an abundant life.

Pick Up Your Sword:

What can we learn from these verses and sayings?

1. *"You are the salt of the earth; but if the salt loses its flavor, how shall it be seasoned? It is then good for nothing but to be thrown out and trampled underfoot by men." ~Matthew 5:13*

   _____

   _____

   _____

2. *"The LORD is my strength and song, And He has become my salvation; This is my God, and I will praise Him; My father's God, and I will exalt Him." ~Exodus 15:2*
   Where will your strength for change come from?

   _____

   _____

   _____

3. *"For you created my inmost being; you knit me together in my mother's womb." ~ Psalms 139:13 (NIV)*
   Who knows best what we are capable of?

   _____

   _____

   _____

4. "Improving your life doesn't have to be about changing everything—it's about making changes that count." ~Oprah Winfrey
   Your thoughts:

   _____

   _____

   _____

<u>Susan B. Anthony</u> **(1820-1906).**

https://www.history.com/topics/womens-history/susan-b-anthony

Anthony played a pivotal role in the women's suffrage movement. In 1878, she and co-workers presented an amendment to Congress that would give women the right to vote. In 1920, Sen. Aaron A. Sargent, R-Calif., introduced the bill and it was ratified as the 19th Amendment to the Constitution.

Lesson 2

Why Define Yourself?

"Don't fear uniqueness.
Fear similarities and acceptance.
Create a new trend by defining yourself."
~ Debasish Mridha

In the art world, new artists begin their journey with simple forms and graduate to more complex styles, mediums, and perspectives. Once they have developed their craft, they then attempt to emulate the great masters of the art world. In this process, artists discover their own styles.

Each great artist, though their techniques may change throughout their careers, has a uniquely recognizable quality. Art lovers can distinguish a Monet from a Renoir, or a Picasso from a Degas. These notable craftsmen have defined themselves and their purpose. They may try out a new style but will generally specialize in one genre of painting. What makes the great artists so extraordinary? They researched, tested, and developed what they did. They spent time and energy returning to the basics and focusing on their strengths. Because the artists narrowed their focus to what they did best, their style is recognizable.

Like the artists, we too must take the time to define who we are. To deny defining ourselves, limits our ability to succeed. We might be moving, but like a treadmill, we are going nowhere. Our personal gifting goes no farther than the end of the rotating belt.

When we are younger, we may try on several talents. Often, we learn more about who we are by failing at who we are not. There will be parts of each trial run that ring true and will be useful when we paint the entire picture of who we are. Life is about becoming; about awakening whoever we are designed to be.

Pick Up Your Sword:

Take a moment to think about who you are:

Read Psalms 139 and note below what rings true to you about you:

"O Lord, You have searched me and known me.
2 You know when I sit down and when I rise up;
You understand my thought from afar.

3 You scrutinize my path and my lying down,
And are intimately acquainted with all my ways.
13 For You formed my inward parts;
You wove me in my mother's womb.
14 I will give thanks to You, for I am fearfully and wonderfully made;
Wonderful are Your works,
And my soul knows it very well.
15 My frame was not hidden from You,
When I was made in secret,
And skillfully wrought in the depths of the earth;

23 Search me, O God, and know my heart;
Try me and know my anxious thoughts;
24 And see if there be any hurtful way in me,
And lead me in the everlasting way.

1. What affirmations do you see about yourself that God declares?

_____

_____

_____

_____

2. *"I will give thanks to You, because I am awesomely and wonderfully made; Wonderful are Your works, and my soul knows it very well." ~ Psalms 139:14*
   What does Psalms 139:14 (NASB) say about who you are?

_____

_____

_____

_____

3. What do you love about you?

_____

_____

_____

_____

4. What don't you love that you can change?

_____

_____

_____

5. What makes you unique?

_____

_____

_____

6. If you knew you could not fail, what changes would you make?

_____

_____

_____

Clara Barton (1821-1912).

https://www.biography.com/people/clara-barton-9200960

Barton founded the American Red Cross and served as its first president. She was a nurse during the Civil War for the Union Army.

Living "Caffeine" or Purpose Driven Lives

"Those who use well what they've been
given even more will be given to them.
But to them who are unfaithful even what
little they have will be taken away."
~Matthew 25:29

Finding your Purpose

Most people are unaware of their inner talents because we do not know what our gifts are, or we have never thought about it before today. To be in-step with who we are and what we spend our life doing, it is vital to know our personal gifting and talents.

Perhaps the job we are doing is not fulfilling, making you feel restless. Could it be that you fell into your current job or were pushed into by someone else's expectations? Maybe you had to take a job to provide for yourself and family but it's not your dream job. First, let me commend you for doing what needs to be done. You are the rock others can build on. Maybe we are living out lives designed for someone else's shoes. Perhaps we're fulfilling an expectation or maybe we just don't know any different. Now might be the right time to move from where we are to where we want to be.

The first step of pursuing passion and purpose in life is understanding what that purpose is. To understand purposefulness and become single-minded we need to know what we were designed to do. God the creator, uniquely designed each of us to influence others with an explicit mission. Knowing that purpose keeps us from stepping on each other's life-jobs and from wandering aimlessly through life. When we are 'off' purpose our lives can feel dissatisfying, unfulfilled, and we may experience a wide variety of downheartedness. Some people will cheerfully do what must be done, yet others find it increasingly difficult to continue in a meaningless fog.

To fill our lives, we often attempt to satisfy our souls with what I call 'caffeine' activities; they satisfy for a while, but soon we need more and more to fill the void. We might throw ourselves into work, fitness, experiences, sex, retail therapy, or a myriad of 'addictions.' But like caffeine, the high soon wears off and we find ourselves living day to day in a survival mode. I don't believe we were created to live in this manner. Scripture tells us we are meant to live a life that is abundant.

When we live our lives abundantly, there is a contagious joy present that births a desire in others to know how to capture the same happiness and purpose. Many of us mistakenly believe our gifts and talents are for us when in fact they are for us to give away. Equipping others to embrace a purposeful life is the reward for understanding and living out our purposes. Defining ourselves is a way of stopping the disgruntled merry-go-round.

God has placed gifts and talents in us.

Summarized from a Joel Olsteen sermon.

"We have potential that we have not begun to use. Too often we have gifts lying dormant because we are not being disciplined to develop them, to grow to become better. We get comfortable. We do not want to stretch…but good enough is not your destiny.

We let thoughts of fear and doubt talk us out of our next level. You are not qualified, . . . etc. . . what if you try and fail? What if you don't allow fear to keep you from your destiny? What if you don't fail?

Don't let another year fly by. Don't miss your due season because of lack of focus and discipline. Don't let fear strangle your desire to be the things you dream about. Life is flying by. You have to draw that line in the sand and say, "I'm going to get focused; I'm going to be intentional; I won't play it safe. I will start stretching…taking steps of faith to grasp these gifts god has given me." Paul says in Romans, that God has given us an ability to do something well. Find out what it is and do it well!

God gives us gifts…He has invested in us…he expects a return on his investment. Do you have gifts that are under-utilized?"

Are you passionate about fulfilling your destiny?

If we are nonchalant about our gifts and talents, then someone else can carry away our blessing. Don't be the person that has the blessing but doesn't value it. Paul told Timothy to stir up your gift—be passionate. The fact that you are reading this, means you are questioning whether you have unused gifts. Do not wait.

You don't have to live worried, as long as you're moving forward. Trying is still forward movement. Only you can take yourself off to the sidelines.

David used to tend sheep and practiced with his slingshot in the field. He became so good at hitting the mark, that when confronted by a giant, his talented slingshot brought down the giant—all 9 feet of him! Perhaps difficult situations we've gone through or are currently going through are designed to strengthen us for a bigger battle. We need to flex our muscles, look for the lesson and be prepared for the next step.

God is not displeased with us because we are flawed, or struggle, he's patiently waiting for us to put our talents to use.

Do your part, get focused, be intentional. Be passionate about your dreams. Step out of your comfort zone. God will increase you more.

Pick Up Your Sword:

1.   God gives us gifts to move us toward our purpose. He has invested in us. He expects a return on His investment. Do you have gifts that are under-utilized?

   _____

2.   Are you taking the time to define your giftings and personality traits to embrace your place in the world?

   _____

3.   If not, why not? What's stopping you?

   _____
   _____
   _____

4.   *"And let us consider how we may spur one another on toward love and good deeds, not giving up meeting together, as some are in the habit of doing, but encouraging one another—and all the more as you see the Day approaching."* ~ *Hebrews 10:24-25*

   What does Hebrews 10:24-25 say about using our gifts? What is our responsibility?

   _____
   _____
   _____
   _____

5.   God is not displeased with us because we are flawed or struggle. He is saddened when we don't use the talent, we already have through Him to serve our purpose for Him. What next step do you need to take to serve your purpose for Him?

   _____
   _____
   _____

Nellie Bly **(1864-1904).**

https://www.biography.com/people/nellie-bly-9216680

A journalist, she launched a new kind of investigative reporting. She is best known for her record-breaking trip around the world by ship in 72 days.

Lesson 4

Spiritual Gifts: Why we are the way we are.

"We have different gifts, according to the grace given to each of us.
If your gift is prophesying, then prophesy in accordance with your faith;
if it is serving, then serve;
if it is teaching, then teach;
if it is to encourage, then give encouragement;
if it is giving, then give generously;
if it is to lead, do it diligently;
if it is to show mercy, do it cheerfully."
~Romans 12:6-8 (NIV)

What is a Spiritual Gift?

Every Christian, upon receiving Christ, has been given a unique set of skills. These are often referred to as gifts, given to serve others. When we do not know our gifting, it is difficult to know our own purposes. Our gifts are specific to each of us. They are meant to build up our families, the church, our communities, and the world.

Proverbs 31:10-11 declares a woman is both highly prized and of great worth, trustworthy and capable. The Hebrew word is specifically reserved to describe a king or highly regarded warriors. You are knit to be this kind of woman.

Knowing your gifting helps embrace God's purpose for you. Equally so, knowing your gifting can help you understand what your purpose is not. The enemy strategizes to keep us ignorant about our true gifting. Serving outside of our best area of influence is his delight. It is common to find people serving in situations they are not skilled to be in. Being out of step with your purpose may cause frustration and rob another person of the ministry they are called to do. Each of us should be serving in the pathway of our unique gift.

Knowing our gifting aligns our spirit with our purpose. Understanding our purpose helps us know where we fit in a group situation. A group made up of all leaders will self-implode. To the contrary, a group with individuals of differing gift sets brings balance and harmony to the team.

We all need goals, a mission, and a strategy. To manage our lives, it's important first to define our skills, passions, and dreams. Your soul needs growth and exploration. Your heart desires purpose and a place to serve and connect. By taking time to evaluate our spiritual gifts, we will be closer to defining our skills, passions, and purpose. Understanding who we are will equip us to know who we are not. Let's start with defining our Spiritual Gifting.

"When I stand before God at the end of my life,
I would hope that I would not have a single bit of talent left,
and could say, 'I used everything you gave me.'"
~Erma Bombeck

The following lesson is created to help you understand your unique gift and how to use it. First take the free test https://gifts.churchgrowth.org/spiritual-gifts-survey/ .

If you include Romans 12, Ephesians 4, and 1 Corinthians 12 together, there are 16 spiritual gifts:

1. Administration
2. Apostleship
3. Discernment
4. Encouraging/ Exhorting
5. Evangelism
6. Faith
7. Giving
8. Hospitality

9. Knowledge
10. Leadership
11. Pastor / Shepherding
12. Prophecy / Perceiving
13. Teaching
14. Serving / Ministry
15. Mercy
16. Wisdom

Pick Up Your Sword:

1. *"Each one should use whatever gift he has received to serve others, faithfully administering God's grace in its various forms." ~1Peter 4:10*
   What does this verse say we should do with our gifts?

   _____

   _____

2. *"The greatest gift of all is love."*
   ~ 1 Corinthians 12:31- 13:3
   What does this mean to you?

   _____

   _____

Giftings : Prophecy, Teaching, administration

Prophecy

Seeing and speaking truth is the core of prophecy. This gift cannot remain quiet when an untruth is heard. They are quick to sense evil, confusion, or spiritual warfare. They see situations as black or white. They want to see injustices made right. Those with the gift of prophecy can discern motives and character. They are bold, cut to the chase, work to create change, and are loyal.

The downside of their passion is they can often be too direct and blunt. Without experience and Christ-like maturity, they can be quick to judge and speak out.

Satan targets prophets because they can be seen as spiritual influencers. This makes them vulnerable for attack. If they fall, many others may fall too. When prophets operate outside of God's direction, they can devastate a wide circle of influence and close relationships.

Teaching

Those with the teaching gift hope to influence change through information. This person works to pass on wisdom and understanding in ways that are easy to follow. Teachers want to teach facts and truths, and love to find facts that perhaps others might have missed; and then share it. Typically, they want to know as much about the topic as possible.

The downside for teachers is they like to present facts but need to work on presenting items in an interesting manner to hold attention. They grow impatient with those who talk a lot but say little. They are rarely impulsive and emotional information does not resonate with them.

Teachers can get stuck on small errors and need to remember to look for the big picture. There is a need to be careful not to fling academic degrees, their resumes, and awards but be alert to God's leading. They must be careful not to teach one thing and live another.

Teachers who respect the word of God are easy to count on because they tend to be self-controlled and dependable.

Administration—leadership—organization

The Greek meaning for this gift is "the one who stands out front." These people can be misunderstood and at times be accused of not being spiritual. These dreamers see the big picture others might not. They have a natural ability to break down large projects into small pieces and then get others involved in the process. They are a great resource for getting projects and people organized. They are great delegators and can see a project through to completion.

Those with the gift of administration welcome constructive criticism and will not fall apart when negatively criticized. They prefer loyalty and love seeing goals accomplished. They hate wasting time and grow weary with those who talk about doing instead of getting the work done. Where no obvious leadership exists, they will rise to the occasion and lead the group.

The downside of this gift is they often do not take time to rest and may take on too much. There is a need to balance work and rest. They always have a 'to do' list and may drive others beyond their gifts and abilities. They need to guard against relying on themselves rather than on God.

Pick Up Your Sword:

1. What do you see as the strengths of these gifts?

   _____

   _____

   _____

2. What do you see as the potential negatives of these gifts?

   _____

   _____

   _____

3. Where can these gifts be used?

   _____

   _____

   _____

Gifts of Service, Mercy and Hospitality

Gift of Service

The gift of service is concerned with meeting practical needs. They are typically hands-on helpers and have an awareness—more than most—of what needs to be done to support others. They are compassionate and cannot help helping. They typically go the extra mile to help someone with extraordinarily little thought to their personal sacrifice.

You can count on the person with the gift of service to do the dirty work others baulk at and they seem to have endless energy to assist. The downside is they can be so helpful that they neglect their family's needs and their own needs. They struggle to set healthy boundaries and often enable others to stay stuck rather than equip them to move forward.

These folks are motivated by praise and appreciation and have a strong desire to be with people.

The more people they meet, the more people they can meet the needs of. They are great team players and are typically extroverts. They are people persons and survive best in short-term projects.

This gift needs to guard against doing so much for others that they do not allow others to do for them. Learning to receive by allowing others to give is tough but vital. They can be too quick to help which may rob the person of the lesson God is teaching. They will need to fight against being so busy that they neglect their own spiritual growth. They must avoid the desire to answer the call of the urgent. This spiritual gift is attentive, friendly, generous, happy, available, and diligent to finish a project.

The Gift of Mercy

The person with the gift of mercy is motivated by love and empathizes with those who do not feel loved. They might appear tough on the outside but are extremely tender-hearted. They are the happy, easy-going person in any group. They are sensitive to other people's happiness or sadness. Those gifted with mercy are also intuitive. They do not have to ask how someone is doing because they already intuitively sense their feelings.

Strongly drawn to those who are lonely, fearful, troubled, or feel ostracized, they want to alleviate their hurt immediately. They may clash with people with the gifts of exhortation or administration feeling they are too impatient or brusque.

Mercy people need friendships. They need to be in relationships that are committed and steadfast. They sense genuine love or lack of it.

They find the good in people when others do not see it. They are quick to extend an emotional hand and to cheer authenticity. They make lifelong friendships and would rather chew off their arm than speak poorly of someone.

The danger is they may not speak up against someone they believe to be wrong or evil. They need to balance their gifting without the emotional rose-colored eyeglasses.

They are attentive, sympathetic, just, kind-hearted, gentle, resilient, and sacrificial. The downside of this gift is they can be too emotional and lose clarity of purpose.

They can be too quick to think people are being too critical or judgmental. They may be too aggressive with trying to help. They may fail to notice when their acts of unconditional caring and authentic help cross a line where others view it as a romantic love. At times, those who receive mercy from a mercy-gifted person may read their help as an expression of sexual desires.

Hospitality

A person with the hospitality gifting thrives bringing others into their home. They love cooking for them and making them feel cared for. Their homes are welcoming places that others find relaxing. They strive to create an atmosphere wherever they are that makes others feel warm, important, safe, and welcomed. They are quick to share their resources, build relationships and allow others to crash at any time in their homes.

Much like the gift of service, hospitality focuses on others first. Scripture even encourages us that when we welcome strangers into our homes, we often are entertaining angels (Hebrews 13:1-2)

The spirit of hospitality is generous and blesses others by providing food, friendship, shelter, and value to a person's spirit.

The upside of this gift is that people are drawn to hospitable people. The challenging part of this gift is knowing how and when to say no. These people-lovers need to understand that if you share a home with other family members, not all of them may have the gift of hospitality and grow weary of constant people traffic.

Pick Up Your Sword:

1. What do you see as the strengths of these gifts?

   _____

   _____

   _____

2. What do you see as the potential negatives of these gifts?

   _____

   _____

   _____

3. Where can these gifts be used?

   _____

   _____

   _____

Exhortation, Giving, Apostleship

Exhortation and Encouragement

Exhorters want to see every believer live an authentic life and prosper on earth and heaven. They desire to see people mature in their relationship in the Lord. They are quick to ask where you are in your spiritual walk. They long for others to live out their full potential.

The person with this gift possesses wisdom, discernment, faith, discretion, authentic love, enthusiasm, and passion. They are the bottom line, logical truth speakers in a group. They may play down or oversimplify a problem a person is having and promise too quickly to fix the situation. They need to learn to empathize rather than blast through to the end goals. There is a need to rein in their strategies to avoid overwhelming a person. Like all giftings, they need to be careful not to step outside of the instructions of Christ and push their own agenda.

The Gift of Giving

This angel wants to give regardless of their financial status. They delight in giving and are willing to share all they have. Giving is not just about money for them. They also share their time, energy, resources, and themselves. Typically, great with money, they make wise investments. They are great bargain hunters and often prefer to give anonymously.

They are eager to inspire others to give to a worthy cause. They catch financial needs that others miss. Many live modest and frugal lives. They do not tend to collect or accumulate things. Unfortunately, they may judge others based on their giving—or lack of giving. They need to be careful not to focus so much on material giving that they neglect spiritual giving. They need to stay away from controlling a ministry because of their gifts and must avoid pressuring others to give like they are able to.

Givers are thrifty, inventive, contented with less, punctual, open-minded, watchful, and typically thankful.

Apostleship

This gifting has a great zeal for missionary work. They delight in traveling to places that have not heard the good news of Christ. They are flexible and resilient with new and differing cultures and are willing to meet new communities on their level. They thrive in mentoring others to plant new churches and to cultivate new Christians in communities that do not have places to worship and grow.

Pick Up Your Sword:

1. What do you see as the strengths of these gifts?

   _____

   _____

   _____

2. What do you see as the potential negatives of these gifts?

   _____

   _____

   _____

3. Where can these gifts be used?

   _____

   _____

   _____

Evangelism, Pastoring, Faith

Evangelism

People with the gift of evangelism are compelled to share the Good News of Christ with others. Talking about the Savior comes naturally for them and they are good at explaining the love of Jesus in simple terms. They love being involved in outreach and missions. They practice the verse "be ready always to give an answer to every man who asks you a reason of the hope that is in you..." (1Peter 3:15)

Pastor and Shepherding

Shepherding or that of a pastor is a call to motivate others to grow in Christ-like ways. They are compelled to lead others in serving the Lord. They lead by example and create an atmosphere to work together. They stress harmony and working together. They see their job as helping others to mature in Christ and work toward the common good of the church. They are most concerned with discerning strengths within the body of believers and build effective teams.

Faith

All Christians have faith in God for their salvation. But those with the gift of faith live without doubt that God cares for them and that faith can move mountains. The gift of faith enables a person to possess an extraordinary amount of belief that God will demonstrate His power, promises and presence in ways that create happiness, peace, and encouragement. Because most of us are pessimistic, the gift of faith is given to some to inspire the rest of us to believe in supernatural blessings. Belief is a choice and is an intellectual process, but faith is a gift of the Holy Spirit—a blessing. Belief comes from the brain; faith comes from the heart and soul. It is an ability to believe God will do what He promises when no one else believes.

Having faith thwarts the enemy. It warns Satan that what he means for evil God can turn to good. The person with the gift of faith needs to stay deeply connected in prayer with Christ and reading daily in the Scriptures is vital.

Pick Up Your Sword:

1. What do you see as the strengths of these gifts?

   _____

   _____

   _____

2. What do you see as the potential negatives of these gifts?

   _____

   _____

   _____

3. Where can these gifts be used?

   _____

   _____

   _____

Discernment, Wisdom

Discernment

The Greek word for discernment is Diakrisis. It means having the ability to discriminate between spirits, the good or evil of them. There is an inborn gut feeling to judge well the moral and practical consequences of decisions. This type of gifting allows the person who possesses it, or those who listen to those people, to avoid costly mistakes or calamity and misadventures. There is also an ability to discern if information from others is from God or out of alignment with righteousness.

The exciting part of this gift is a person who discerns evil can warn others or call them out if they are leading others astray. Soaked in the love and wisdom of Christ, discernment can be quite valuable in the church, the family, and their circle of influence.

If the person strays from the Lord, the negative pendulum swing of this gift can be an arrogance or self-serving attitude. In this event, the gifting can become tainted and/or create false discernment and anxiety. Staying connected to the word and prayer is vital.

Wisdom

The gift of wisdom in the Greek language is Sophia and refers to the intimate understanding of God's word. Understanding is the heart of this gift. It brings about concrete acts of love. It is the ability to instinctively receive insight on how knowledge can best be applied to group situations or individuals. This knowledge helps others make sound decisions, discern God's will and to grow closer with Christ. Godly wisdom releases us from fear and gives us strength to face difficult situations. When life flattens us, wisdom restores our faith and courage.

For wisdom to be useful it is vital to live an upright life to maintain the utterance of wisdom.

Pick Up Your Sword:

1. What do you see as the strengths of these gifts?

   _____

   _____

   _____

2. What do you see as the potential negatives of these gifts?

   _____

   _____

   _____

3. Where can these gifts be used?

   _____

   _____

   _____

Which Gift is the Best?

> *"Everybody can be great...because anybody can serve.*
> *You don't have to have a college degree to serve.*
> *You don't have to make your subject and verb agree to serve.*
> *You only need a heart full of grace. A soul generated by love."*
> *~Martin Luther King, Jr.*

One gift is not superior to another. Each is given as God sees fit. Gifts are given to build up and benefit a group of people created to work together. There are gifts that feel 'showy' or ones that we might prefer. That is not the way God created them. Each gift is designed to work in conjunction with all the others to the benefit of the whole body.

If we read further into the next Lesson (1Corinthians 13) we will see that above all else, each gift should be used in love to edify others rather than ourselves. In fact, we are warned that if we do not use our gifts with love, we cease to be a positive influencer. We become a noisy gong.

1Corinthians 13

"13 If I speak with the tongues of mankind and of angels, but do not have love, I have become a noisy gong or a clanging cymbal. ² If I have the gift of prophecy and know all mysteries and all knowledge, and if I have all faith so as to remove mountains, but do not have love, I am nothing. ³ And if I give away all my possessions to charity, and if I surrender my body so that I may glory, but do not have love, it does me no good.

⁴ Love is patient, love is kind, it is not jealous; love does not brag, it is not arrogant. ⁵ It does not act disgracefully, it does not seek its own benefit; it is not provoked, does not keep an account of a wrong suffered, ⁶ it does not rejoice in unrighteousness, but rejoices with the truth; ⁷ it keeps every confidence, it believes all things, hopes all things, endures all things.

⁸ Love never fails; but if there are gifts of prophecy, they will be done away with; if there are tongues, they will cease; if there is knowledge, it will be done away with. ⁹ For we know in part and prophesy in part; ¹⁰ but when the perfect comes, the partial will be done away with. ¹¹ When I was a child, I used to speak like a child, think like a child, reason like a child; when I became a man, I did away with childish things. ¹² For now we see in a mirror dimly, but then face to face; now I know in part, but then I will know fully, just as I also have been fully known. ¹³ But now faith, hope, and love remain, these three; but the greatest of these is love."

Pick up your sword:

1. After studying and discovering your spiritual gift, what does Lesson 13 instruct us as to the most important gift?

   _____

   _____

   _____

2. What is your spiritual gift? _____

3. Are you using it? _____

4. If so, how? If not, why not? _____

   _____

   _____

   _____

   _____

"Dare to love yourself as if you were a rainbow,
with gold at both ends."
~ Aberjhani

Amelia Earhart (1897-1939).

https://www.ameliaearhart.com/biography/

Earhart, the first female aviator to fly solo across the Atlantic Ocean, received the U.S. Distinguished Flying Cross for her accomplishments. Earhart and her navigator, Fred Noonan, disappeared in 1937 over the central Pacific Ocean while attempting to fly around the globe.

Lesson 5

Learning Styles

"I have never let schooling interfere
with my education."
~ Mark Twain

What is a Learning Style?

A learning Style is how our brains record information for retrieval for later. We are born with a dominate learning style and a secondary style that works in tandem. Although we may pass through many learning styles as we mature chronologically, we favor one style over the others. Infants and toddlers tend to use a tactile style of taking in information. Tactile means we have a need to feel everything. You have probably observed a little one putting every item within their reach into their mouth. As children develop, they become experiential or kinesthetic learners.

The kinesthetic learner does best by doing or experiencing information. This is the 'exploration' or 'discovery' phase of growth. Once we become a teenager, our learning style has most likely become predominate in 80%-90% of our information processing. As adults, we have finely tuned our predominant style and supporting it with a secondary style. We may dabble in other learning styles but typically resort back to our first and second styles.

There are 4 basic learning styles:

1. Visual learners
2. Auditory learners
3. Verbal Learners
4. Kinesthetic or Experiential Learners

Visual Learners

Visual learners take in information through sight. They are the ones that will remember colors, vivid pictures of events, posters, etc. It is like living with a camera always taking pictures.

Visual learners' strengths:

- Prefer directions that are written and take detailed notes for information recall.
- Tend to think in pictures and grasp the big picture readily.
- Will notice the pictures, posters, etc. in a room.
- Can recall diagrams, charts, and words after only seeing them a few times.
- They tend to be puzzle people, love to read, write, and often are the keepers of the family   stories they have witnessed.
- Love parables, analogies, can visually put together abstract figures.
- Able to look at the pictures on a direction sheet and put together something rather than read the directions.
- Great at directions because they hold a mental 'map' in their heads.
- Love organization and things put away in the same place every time. Order creates restfulness, calm and a sense of security for them.
- If desks or rooms are a mess, they know where every pile is and what's in it.
- When reading for details they can often recall which side of the page and where on the page the information can be found.
- Strong spatial intelligence and can clearly see a 'what it could be' completed project.
- Love colors, lines, art, and fashion. They have an instinct for style or creating atmosphere.
- Dream in color, like charts and understand them easily.
- Prefer to work in a quiet room alone.
- When trying to remember something they often visualize a picture for easier recall.
- When others would run from the work, they often find it relaxing to organize closets, drawers, files, etc.
- Prefer to sit in front of a room, theater, lecture, etc. to avoid the distraction of others in their line of vision which may become the priority focus.

The disadvantage for visual learners:

- Taken to an extreme, their skills at seeing what could be are so strong they fail to see what is. You have probably met the eternal optimist that is inspiring, but they may struggle with the realities of life.

- These concept rich learners are bored easily with frill or filler material.
- They are excellent spellers but often cannot remember names.
- They often need to see a speaker's body language and facial expressions to understand concept content given in oral form and can misinterpret this information.

Auditory Learners

Auditory learners learn through hearing. They are the children who only need to be told once. They are the students who typically do very well in a traditional school setting where the days are spent sitting and listening. As adults, they are great multi-taskers and project managers for companies that meet to discuss verbally plans for the future.

They rarely speak unless they are certain they have their information correct or have something profound to say. Auditory learners are excellent people observers and often are the ones who rescue friends because they are such good listeners. The good news is auditory learners retain about 70% of what they hear. The bad news is only about 30% of people are auditory learners. Unfortunately, typical educational situations are designed for visual and auditory students. Which means in a classroom of thirty, only nine students will be grasping the information, which leaves twenty-one students lost or distracting others.

Auditory learners' strengths:

- Love engaging in group discussions and can remember what they as well as the rest of the group says.
- Can recite back oral instructions or conversations from 6 months to a year ago. You only need to tell them once.
- Excel at lectures, online audio classes, audio books, any information shared orally.
- Can memorize large portions of text when it is given to them in pieces orally.
- Have a need to discuss their perceptions or things they do not understand which can be very beneficial to the student too shy to speak up.
- Make wonderful musicians, often repeating music by playing by ear, can memorize anything put to a rhythm or song.

The disadvantages for auditory learners:

- If you misstate something, you will be reminded of it. They do not forget.
- Repetition drives them nuts. They get it the first time.
- They have a need to discuss things they do not understand, which can cause them to appear disruptive to others.
- Easily distracted by noise. Since they learn through their ears, they are always aware of every conversation around them.

Verbal Learners

A child who is a verbal learner must speak and hear themselves speak for information to become logged into memory. Consequently, this child does not do well in a sit-down and listen to the learning situation. If you are going to lecture this child, you need to keep the points short and clear and always ask – Now tell me what you heard or what you think I said. And have them list it back to you. You can start with one or two points when they are younger. By the teen years, if you keep directions simple, you should be able to give them a 4–5-point message. As adults, they'll need to discuss the directions and use their secondary learning style to retain the information.

Verbal learners' strengths:

- Prefer oral instruction that they can verbally engage in.
- Typically have highly developed auditory skills and can concentrate on one person even in a crowded room of distraction if they are being engaged with words.
- Their vocabulary is typically more advanced, and they speak with eloquence and clarity early on. When learning to read, they can retain the 'content' even though they are still decoding words.
- In a classroom or group setting, this student CAN talk and listen at the same time!
- They think in words rather than pictures.

The disadvantages for verbal learners:

- They are great at verbal debates—If you engage them in a verbal battle without being this type of learning style, expect to be frustrated or be reduced to yelling.

- In a classroom setting, the student can talk and listen at the same time, but most students lack this skill and style.

- Written information can often have extraordinarily little meaning if it is not combined with verbal lecture, instruction, and discussion.

- When focusing on reading or writing, they can be easily distracted by noise (because they process by hearing, any extra noise will become the priority.)

- May seem to be distracted processing through their own filter when others are talking with them. Although they are great listeners, they are searching internally for a form of reference.

- They interpret underlying meanings through non-verbal cues such as speed, inflection, tone, and pitch, often misinterpreting meaning.

Kinesthetic Learners or Hands on Learners

Kinesthetic learners learn by experiencing, handling, trial, and error rather than reading, writing, or hearing and talking about events. Hands-on learners have the greatest potential to embrace new concepts if their learning means are not stifled. They ask more questions and understand the full concept of science and math. I always loved teaching kinesthetic learners, but it does require major preparedness, and staying two steps ahead of them. But when they get a concept, they get it so well they can teach it to the next student.

Kinesthetic learners' strengths:

- Learn best while moving—it is essential to keep the body occupied while the brain is attempting to log data entry for future retrieval.

- Can recall rote memorization if they have written it a few times, but best if they can connect an experience with it.

- Can recall the feelings of memory, story, or event better than the details of such. They may know they were scared but cannot tell you why.

- Have a strong ability to manipulate objects skillfully.

- Typically, outstanding athletes or any skill that requires precise movement, balance, and eye-hand coordination.

- Usually learn best by using their hands or body.

- Strong at computers due to the ability to tactilely manipulate it.

The disadvantages for kinesthetic learners:

- Generally, more difficult to focus their attention in a sitting environment (unless the situation is interactive) but once they are focused, it is equally difficult to disengage them.

- Hearing and talking does not make the information 'real' to these learners.

- This style typically learns what to do by failing first and then completing the tasks successfully. They prefer trial and error learning.

- They may have difficulty retaining information from reading because they remember less what they have seen or what was talked about.

- Generally poor spellers.

- They tend to process physically, which could become aggressive if not taught how to communicate verbally.

- They tend to be falsely accused of being a slow learner.

- They tend to have a lot of physical contact which can be either annoying or misinterpreted in a group setting.

- Can sometimes have trouble associating words to feelings.

Pick Up Your Sword:

1. Have your figured out your primary learning style? What is it?

   _____

   _____

2. What do you think is your secondary style?

   _____

   _____

3. How will this new information change the way you retain information?

   _____

   _____

<u>Jessie Benton Fremont</u> **(1824-1902).**

https://en.wikipedia.org/wiki/Jessie_Benton_Fr%C3%A9mont

Fremont was a writer and political activist. She was considered the brains behind her husband, John C. Fremont, and his famous exploration westward. She turned his notes into readable books and made connections in Washington, D.C., that eventually made him famous.

Lesson 6

Love Languages

"The beginning of love is to let those we love be perfectly themselves,
And not to twist them to fit our own image.
Otherwise,
We love only the reflection of ourselves we find in them."
~Thomas Merton

Knowing how we love and how we feel loved goes a long way to understanding our needs. In Gary Chapman's book The Five Love Languages (https://www.amazon.com/Love-Languages-Secret-that-Lasts/dp/080241270X/ ref=sr_1_1?dchild=1&keywords=five+love+languages&qid=1625697570&sr=8-1) he outlines how people express and experience love. These five languages are: acts of service, gift giving, physical touch, quality time and words of affirmation. Let's take a short look at each one:

Acts of service: People who feel loved through acts of service need to see love demonstrated. Words matter little, but actions speak volumes. They feel loved when someone sees a task and does it for them. They feel jilted by broken commitments and general non-helpfulness. If you are this love language, be aware that the other person may not know this, and you may feel let down or ignored; neither of which may be true. Likewise, if you have a relationship (spouse, child, parent, etc.) that has this love language no amount of saying, "I love you," will replace their sense of 'I'm important enough for you to do things for.'

Words of Affirmation: For these people words speak louder than actions. Hearing is believing for them. The best assurance of love is saying, "I love you because . . . " and fill in the blanks. They need to hear it often. Be wary of harsh words or name-calling, you can crush their spirit. Speaking your pride, confidence or love authentically are words taken directly to their hearts. If you are with an individual who doesn't speak emotions well, you may feel unloved. Likewise, if you are a parent, spouse, friend of someone with this language you need to be attentive to texting, cards, and frequent compliments.

Receiving Gifts: This love language can get a bad rap making the receiver look materialistic, however demonstrating gift giving to the receiver is less about the dollar amount and more about the fact that the gift was thought out and unique to them. It says you cared enough to spend time searching for something meaningful to them. They take birthdays, holidays, and special moments very seriously and like to mark them with special trinkets denoting a memory. If you have a relationship that this is their love language, note what they tell you matters to them. Keep a list of things they've said they would like. Likewise, if you are this love language, be certain you explain to the other person that the dollar amount is not the main importance . . . ,it is the thought that counts.

Quality time: This person is touched by time spent with them. It says to them that you would rather be with them than anywhere else. This individual wants to know that what they think, and feel are important to their partners. Group dates don't count for them. If you are committed to this type of person, clearly putting in the time—unrushed, simple, and easy—says they are a priority. Ways to show quality time is to make eye contact, unrushed conversation with no agenda, and shared experiences. Turn off the TV and cell phone and share moments together. Be careful not to look at your watch or squeeze them into your schedule so they don't feel the 'time limit'. If you are this love language, your partner may not realize their working 60 hours a week to support the family feels more like you are married to the job rather than wanting to be with you.

Physical Touch: This love language might sound like it's all about sex, but it is far more than just sex. It is the simple touches, back rub, hand holding that says, "I love you and want to be near you." They are huggers. When their partners are not physically demonstrative, they can feel unloved and lonely. A simple hand on the small of their back, stroking the back of their hand and rubbing their hair can all be physical signs of love. Be careful to meet these needs or there can be many other places they may receive this attention. If this is your love language be certain to have strong boundaries in place to avoid touch outside your relationship.

Take this Love Language's test: Click Here

(https://www.5lovelanguages.com/quizzes/couples-quiz/)

What is your love language? _____

What is your significant other's? _____

What is your best friend's? _____

What are your family members' love languages?

Name   language

_____

_____

_____

_____

_____

_____

Knowing each person's love language in your circle of relationships will allow you to meet 'love' needs. For instance, if your child's love language is quality time and you give them gifts or words of affirmation, they may feel short-changed. Generally, we tend to love people the way that we feel loved missing opportunities to gird up others' love buckets.

Make it fun to take the test with others or become a keen observer of what inspires them. Take the time to understand each love language and each person in your family. Check out the author's site: The 5 Love Languages (https://www.5lovelanguages.com/resources/books/)

Understanding your own love language will equip you to ask for what you need.

Amanda Gorman, (1998- Present),

https://www.theamandagorman.com/

at 22 years of age became the first young poet to recite "The Hill We Climb" at the Presidential Inauguration. A poet and activist writes on issues of oppression, feminism, race, and marginalization.

Lesson 7

Defining Your Energy

"The energy of the mind is the essence of life."
~Aristotle

The badass lifestyle is a life lived to the best of who you are designed to be. When all the parts line up, we are influential, proactive, and intentional. We respond rather than react and make decisions from seeing the whole picture. A badass woman knows her boundaries, her personality type, her priorities and her worth. She understands her strengths and weaknesses and uses them to the best of her ability. She does not apologize for who she is, she does not move through life haphazardly, and does not live life putting out fires because she is not prepared.

There is a peace in knowing who you are, and what your purpose is. You can accept or decline distractions dressed up like opportunities. Understanding who you are creates a confidence that destroys the need to be a people-pleaser or living your life by the seat of your pants.

Living on purpose means we need to explore, understand, and accept our personality traits, our unique talents and gifts and understand our limitations.

Energy levels

Are you a high energy person? Or do you need to pace yourself more? Are you a morning person or a night owl? This might sound strange but knowing when your energy is at its highest or lowest can make a huge difference in your productivity.

For instance, I front load my week, then wind down toward the weekend. I could work out in the morning, but it is never the intensity that I can perform mid-afternoon. I must be careful that my day does not push into my self-care but the idea of sweating first thing in the morning is abhorrent to me.

I am most productive later in the day. Once all my household jobs are done, I can dig into my creative side. Forcing myself to work outside my energy level can cause me to spend an hour doing a ten-minute job. Likewise, working long hours on a Friday means I am trudging through burn out hours. My clients know I am not available from noon on Friday until 9am Monday morning. It took me a long time to figure this out about myself, but it has paid off tremendously.

Personality traits

Are you an introvert or an extrovert? Neither is right or wrong but knowing who you are helps to determine what job, social activities, energy expenditures you have in you. Instead of fighting yourself, you can begin to plan your social strategies.

Covid-19 locked us all at home to stay safe. For many, lock-down was a relief and long needed projects got finished. But for others staying home felt like a prison sentence. Isolation for an extrovert is painful. Understanding our natural personality bents can go a long way to internal peace.

If you are an extrovert, you are most comfortable in group settings gathering friends to you. You gain energy being in group activities. Being around people makes you feel alive and skipping home missing them the moment they are out of your site. You limit your alone time and are the one who most often keeps a group together through events and communication.

If you are an introvert, you are comfortable on your own. You do not feel a pressing need to be 'involved' in groups. You are much more selective about who you spend time with and how often. You love people but social events drain you. Introverts are good company for themselves and covet entire days alone. Introverts love people but will not be skipping home if they have too many group social activities on the calendar.

Introverts do not understand extroverts' needs to be signed up for several activities a week. And extroverts can feel rejected by an introvert when they do not want to join in as often.

Then there are the blends of both. An introvert that gains energy from perhaps teaching or speaking to groups, loves people, but will need a couple days of solace following group events. An extrovert will be bored silly with too much down time and will be looking for the next thing they can do. The world needs both, but we need to know which we are.

I am an introvert with a passion for people. Odd combination huh? I am built to want to 'fix' situations and can clearly see the steps between where people are and where they tell me they want to be. At times, I wish I could turn this 'gift' off, but it is knit into the very fiber of who I am. For me, being in a group of people often can be exhausting because I wrestle between helping and reining in this skill. I do far better in one-on-one conditions and 'one-to-many' situations. I used to think there was something wrong with me when I avoided group settings and large social gatherings until I discovered my personality strengths. I love group situations but need alone time to recharge and caring about people is a strength that needs boundaries.

Introverts have a several tiered circle of relationships. Imagine if you will a bullseye. The first circle closest to the center is reserved for intimate relationships (your husband, your kids, your family, --they have instant access to you). The next wider circle is for close relationships—your close friends, trusted associations. The next wider circle is for associations and contacts. They may be people you work with, clients, people you like but would not vacation with. An introvert's first and second circle are limited, and then grows larger as you move out to the outer rings. Where the extrovert differs is their second circle of influence may be much larger—perhaps the size of the introverts 3 and 4th rings.

Again, there is nothing wrong with either, but understanding who you are will help determine what areas of service and involvement will make you happy.

Right brain or left brain?

Understanding your dominate thinking power is vital to determining what kinds of jobs and activities will find you at your best. Right brain dominant people tend to be creative, concept people. They need their souls fed and find various was to solve that hunger. They tend to be less organized, or goal driven. You have often heard them called B-type personalities or laid-back individuals.

Left brain people tend to be planners, organizers and lovers of math, science, logic, and order. They are typically goal driven. They are more likely disciplined and enjoy tackling difficult problems for the joy of finding a solution. They desire having a purpose and striving for it. They are often called A-type personalities.

Again, neither are right or wrong, but understanding which you are can explain a lot to you or go a long way to understanding others you associate with. Attempting to be something you are not will only frustrate you and cause you to miss-step decisions. For example: An A type person would be a good choice for organizing and administrating where a B type individual might be overwhelmed by the same position. A B-type personality could be amazingly comfortable in an unstructured situation and not feel a need to 'fix' or organize it. It is painful for an A-type person to 'fly by the seat of their pants', they want to know the end goal, time limit and resources available so they can plan. We need both individuals.

Pick Up Your Sword:

1. What is your best energy time?

   _____

2. Are you an introvert or an extrovert?

   _____

3. Are you a right-brain person or a left-brain individual?

   _____

4. *"Whatever you do, work at it with all your heart, as working for the Lord, not for men." ~Colossians 3:23*

   What does this verse mean to you based on the information you've learned about yourself in numbers 1-3?

   _____

   _____

   _____

5. How will this information change what and how you serve?

   _____

   _____

   _____

<u>Marguerite Higgins</u> **(1920-1966).**

http://biography.yourdictionary.com/marguerite-higgins

Higgins was a reporter and war correspondent for the New York Herald Tribune during WWII, the Korean War, and the Vietnam War. She advanced the cause of equal opportunity for female war correspondents and was the first woman awarded a Pulitzer Prize for Foreign Correspondence in 1951.

The Seasons in a Woman's Life

"Be a first-rate version of yourself,
not a second-rate version of someone else."
~Judy Garland

The saying goes, "Age is just a number." I believe it is more than that, it is a state of mind. There are seasons in a woman's life, and we need to embrace the one we are in. There are roughly four seasons that we pass through:

Spring: Birth to mid-twenties. This is the time in our lives where we are being nourished, educated, and exploring all things new. It is a time for focusing on ourselves and discovering what we want out of life, as well as exploring our potential purpose.

This is a season of making mistakes and trying and failing. Discovery is the name of the game as we shape our characters and begin to format our futures.

We need to be taking advantage of every opportunity that is not permanently scarring or fatal. Say yes to as many opportunities as possible. Be intentional with activities. Trust your gut instincts—if it does not feel right or positive for you, walk away. Engage in activities on purpose that build confidence, self-esteem, and new experiences. Begin now to set healthy boundaries that protect your mind, your heart, and your body. Take time to be still. There is much to consider, and mind-wandering is essential to understanding what you think and feel.

Summer: (mid-twenties to mid-forties)

This is a time in your life for rewards, celebrations, and purpose. This season is about choosing paths for your life such as careers, getting married, building a family. It is a great time to begin setting goals or creating a bucket list of events you want to accomplish. This is a time to ask the hard questions: Who am I? Who do I want to be? What do I have to do to be that person? How far am I from that goal? What will my legacy be? This season is for starting new activities, searching for jobs you prefer or are interested in making a career, and building lasting relationships rather than doing what you had to do in the spring season to move forward.

This season brings about experience and some wisdom for taking risks for things you are passionate about. You have gained self-confidence and courage and are less distracted by emotional fatigue. You can maneuver through this season by being prepared for future events. Take the time to know who you are and your purpose. Being more mature, your decisions need to be more researched, planned and less seat-of-your pants impulsive. This season may include others that your decisions will affect so planning well will prevent mis-directions.

Take advantage of seasoned mentors and opportunities to grow personally, spiritually, and career wise.

Fall: (mid-forties to mid-sixties)

Autumn is a season for reflecting on past missteps and dealing with them head on. It is a time to consider survival for the future. Perhaps your momentum for 'bucket list' items is waning, and now is the time to revive them. This season is the perfect time to become the Titus woman who reaches out to mentor other women not quite as far down the path as you are. Your experiences can be vital to avoid pitfalls for others. It is also a time to reap the rewards of the planning and hard work you have done in the first two seasons of your life. It is a time to gather friends and family and lean into enjoying these precious moments. You may still be raising children, and now also caring for older parents. This season can also be known as the 'sandwich' season. You are probably still working and splitting your time between adult children, grandchildren, and aging parents. There may be times of loss with family and friends that will test your strength and stamina.

Embracing this season, you may enjoy new dreams, realizing old dreams like travel and new careers or even no career. You may be living a lifestyle that answers the past seasons question, "Now what?" Your age will inspire you to feel more contentment, gratitude, and a sense of satisfaction. You will like more about you than in your past seasons, and not take yourself so seriously. You will worry less what others think about you and focus more on what you think of you. Be sure to spend time taking care of yourself, investing in relationships, and checking off bucket items. Take time to go to lunch with friends, change your outlook, and enjoy a sunrise or sunset. Buy that RV and travel. Do what you have always talked about doing and embrace each memory. Build experiences over things.

Winter: (mid-sixties to end of life)

When life turns to winter, it makes us remember and long for the past. However, this is equally a time to make a new new. This season can come with loss, health challenges and waning purpose but how you handle it can also be your greatest swan song.

You are probably slowing down a bit which makes you a perfect place for a grandchild or great grandchild to land. You may be the listening ear for a struggling teen, neighbor, or peer who has suffered loss. Life may be changing quickly around you but saying yes to new opportunities is still the strongest way to maneuver life.

You have the experience needed to weather most storms, and the wise counsel for others who have not. Naps, tea, and a good book are life's treats to embrace for the day. Volunteering, sharing ideas, networking and entertaining are all gifts of this season.

These seasons of life are guidelines for embracing and then moving through transitions. Recognizing which season, we are in may help to alleviate our frustration that we should be doing more. When we are at the business of raising babies, it might not be the best time to have your energies scattered. Perhaps running for a political office is best saved for the fall of our lives when family is grown, and we have more time to devote.

I want to encourage the summer season to NOT buy into the pressures of the world that tells us we can have it all. You can, but there is a price to pay for attempting to have it all at the same time. Just like any project, even if we are highly organized, splitting focus means something (or someone) gets less than 100% attention. That means setting priorities and boundaries, so we know what gets our first attention, second attention and so on. I am not an advocate of quality time makes up for quantity of time. You cannot embrace a great exercise routine on Monday and expect to get the same results if you exercised five days a week, no matter how great a workout Monday was.

None of the things we have discussed have a right or wrong to them with one exception: if you are standing in someone else's season, you are missing out on the fullness of who you are or are meant to be.

Wearing someone else's lifestyle or personality or purpose will cause restless dissension in your spirit. You will continue to be 'stuck' in someone else's interpretation of who you are. The world will be missing your uniqueness, and you may miss your calling in life.

Why am I so passionate about equipping women to discover their badass within? Because when you step out there and discover your strengths, find your voice and purpose, not only the world wins, your circle of influence wins, and you will settle into a quiet place of strength, peace, and an unshakeable knowledge that you are doing what you were designed do. When it is right, it feels like breathing. It sets your soul free in such a way you will feel excited and blessed to move through life day to day.

Being in sync with yourself, your talents, your personality and giftings is like winning the lottery, or the exuberance of falling in love, or witnessing a miracle. It is your soul's way of saying, "I'm here, this is me and I know what I'm doing is what I was meant to do."

Pick Up Your Sword:

1. What season are you in?

   _____

   _____

2. Are there places in your life where you are living 'out of season'?

   _____

   _____

3. Where are you out of sync with you? What can you do to align yourself?

   _____

   _____

4. Do you have moments of time for self-perspective?

   _____

   _____

5. If not, what can you do to take some time for yourself?

   _____

   _____

<u>Grace Hopper</u> **(1906-1992).**

https://en.wikipedia.org/wiki/Grace_Hopper

A computer scientist and Navy rear admiral, Hopper played an integral role in creating programs for some of the world's first computers.

Bad Day or Spiritual Warfare?

"For our struggle is not against flesh and blood,
but against the rulers, against the authorities,
against the powers of this dark world and
against the spiritual forces of evil in the heavenly realms."
~Ephesians 6:12

Spiritual Warfare

What is it? Anyone who has received Christ as savior becomes an enemy to the enemy. Our enemy does not take time off. We're told he goes about seeking people to devour. If the devil wore a red suit and carried a pitchfork, we would be more aware of his efforts. Instead, his wiles are much more subtle—more like a whisper than a roar. Our enemy works so understatedly clever most of us miss the day-to-day stumbles.

It might look like:

- Frequent fear, anxiety, and lack of faith

- Anger triggered by little things.

- Past guilt – not accepting God's forgiveness.

- Holding on to bitterness

- Jealousy, self-righteousness

- Lack of self-esteem and confidence

- Fear of change

- Conflict, disagreement, and tension in relationships

- Self-loathing

A typical conversation with people regarding Satan is often met with disbelief or a Hollywood version of who he is. Or people are fearful and feel the topic is too unnerving to talk about. But Scripture warns us if we ignore the powerful deceits and charms of the devil is unrealistic and dangerous. We cannot go to battle unprepared. Our best armor of defense is to understand where and how the enemy operates and then gird ourselves in wisdom and prayer.

Why do we fall into the path of Satan's grasp? We often fail to recognize our enemy's strategies. We let our emotions get ahold of us rather than standing on the words of Christ. Our prayer time lacks, we don't know our bibles, or we get led astray by someone that 'looks' like they know what to do. We are often like lambs to slaughter.

The good news is we have an advocate more powerful than the deceiver that never sleeps—the Holy Spirit.

First, let's define a crisis. It's different from person to person and from day to day. The truth is a real crisis borders on being a catastrophe, a calamity, a disaster, or an emergency. That's the moment we need to react and allow the fight-or-flight hormones to take over.

More often today, what we call a crisis might just be a necessary confrontation, a surprised disagreement, procrastination, predicament, a need for clarity, or a personality clash. Instead of war, it's a skirmish.

Could be:

- We're unprepared.

- We haven't taken responsibility prior to the situation.

- Our perception is off.

- We misunderstand.

- We're scared.

- We're overwhelmed.

- We're defensive unnecessarily.

- We've never defined how we feel about the situation.

- We'd rather not face the truth.

- We have unreal expectations.

- We haven't truthfully communicated our needs (maybe we don't know what they are)

One of the things I've learned (not that I have this perfected) is to ask myself five questions to help me respond:

1. Am I over-tired, stressed, or hormonal and reacting instead of responding?
   a. If the answer is Yes, then stop, wait, handle this another day.
   b. If the answer is No, move on to question #2.

2. Am I taking myself too seriously?
   a. If the answer is Yes, then stop, wait, analyze more, then handle this another day.
   b. If the answer is No, then move on to question #3.

3. What can I learn from this? What am I going through that might be valuable to me or others in the future?

4. How do I pass this lesson on?

5. Who do I pass this lesson on to?

Reactions can be a positive emotion. We all enjoy the pure laughter of a child, and the gut reaction to a well-timed comedic punchline. But over-reacting to an unkind comment or a tense situation gives away our power to manage the situation.

We've all said things we wish we could take back or that we were sorry for the moment the words left our mouth. Then we must swallow our pride and apologize, hoping to repair the relationship.

If we can learn to take a slow deep breath before we assess the situation, then assume the best before we speak, we can preserve our power and dignity. By responding wisely, we earn the right to speak wisdom into others' lives. It might just be that our carefully selected words—even in a situation where more people would not do well—may inspire character growth rather than leave lasting scars.

We cannot stop the wind from blowing, but we can set our sails in such a way as to respond to the wind.

Pick Up Your Sword:

1. *"The reason the Son of God appeared was to destroy the devil's work."*
   ~1John 3:8
   Why did God come?

   _____

   _____

2. Look up the following verses and tell what the scriptures says of the devil:
   Matthew 12:24 _____
   Matthew 4:3 _____
   Revelation 12:10 _____
   Genesis 3:1 _____
   Isaiah 54:16 _____
   Peter 5:8 _____
   Matthew 13:39 _____
   Samuel 16:14 _____

3. *"But you, O Lord, are a shield about me, my glory, and the lifter of my head."*
~Psalms 3:3
When we are fearful of Satan's evil, what do these verses promise?

_____

_____

4. *"My God, my rock, in whom I take refuge, my shield, and the horn of my salvation, my stronghold and my refuge, my savior; you save me from violence." ~ 2 Samuel 22:3 (ESV)*

_____

_____

5. *"The God of peace will soon crush Satan under your feet. The grace of our Lord Jesus Christ be with you." ~ Romans 16:20*

_____

_____

6. *"What then shall we say to these things? If God is for us, who can be against us?" ~Romans 8:31*

_____

_____

7. *"No temptation has overtaken you that is not common to man. God is faithful, and he will not let you be tempted beyond your ability, but with the temptation he will also provide the way of escape, that you may be able to endure it." ~ 1 Corinthians 10:13-14*

_____

_____

8. *"Trust in the Lord with all your heart, do not lean on your own understanding. In all your ways acknowledge him, and he will make straight your paths." ~ Proverbs 3:5-6*

_____

_____

9. *"We know that everyone who has been born of God does not keep on sinning, but he who was born of God protects him, and the evil one does not touch him." ~ 1 John 5:18*

_____

_____

<u>Alethea Gibson</u>, **(1927-2003),**

https://www.history.com/topics/black-history/althea-gibson

dominated the American Tennis Association circuit at 15 years old. She broke the tennis color barrier at Forest Hills Country Club U.S. Open and the following year became the first African American to play at Wimbledon. Later, she broke the same rules as a professional golfer. She paved the athletic pathways for future women of color.

Spiritual Warfare –Running toward the battle!

"You have to expect spiritual warfare
whenever you stand up for righteousness
or call attention to basic values.
It's just a matter of light battling the darkness.
But the light wins every time.
You can't throw enough darkness on light to put it out."
~Thomas Kinkade

Why do we need to love spiritual warfare? Most of us would rather run the other direction, but those who stick and stay, weathering the storms learn important battle strategies designed to win the next war.

Hardships come our way to mature us. If we do not handle situations well the first time staying in the fight will give us a winning perspective for the next time. Warfare humbles us. It reminds us we cannot fight every fight alone. Warfare trains us to use the strength that comes from the intimate knowledge of God.

Conflict teaches us we have a place to turn to and to hide behind. When we come against something that is impossible to handle, we can watch God handle the skirmish far better than we ever could. Flexing these muscles builds strength and reveals character flaws we need to build.

Conflict enlightens our weaknesses and gives opportunity to build new strengths. Wins against the enemy equip us with confidence to go into future battles. And wins with God in control blesses and encourages us.

What gets in our way to winning the wars? The short answer: fear, selfishness, control, and pride. Let's look at each one:

Fear keeps us from engaging in any battle. When fear replaces faith –I'm not good enough, I'm not smart enough, etc.—we rob ourselves of discovering our internal strength. When David met Goliath (the giant) all he had on him was a sling shot and a stone, but he trusted what he was about to do would honor God and in one shot he killed the evil threatening his people. We need Goliath faith to fight against our giants.

Selfishness keeps us focused on our own needs and robs us of the understanding of other's desires. In a self-centered state we are not available beyond the end of our noses. We miss opportunities to be an answer to prayer and perhaps discover our own purpose. When we are 'other' focused, we may discover golden nuggets within ourselves.

Control is the disguised monster to faithlessness. We falsely believe if we are in control of every situation, we will avoid hurt or manipulation. And worse yet, no one wants to be controlled by others! We don't like it and others don't revel in it when we do it to them. It is hard work controlling everyone and every situation. It's exhausting! It might be time to restfully watch God do what he knows is best for us.

Pride says I know more than you and sucks us into the selfishness of needing control. God wants us to love people the way they are rather than the way we want them to be. When conflicts occur instead of a stand-off try these Joyce Meyer magic words, "I think I'm right, but I could be wrong."

It's difficult to give up control of our lives whether it is out of fear, pride, or past hurts. The good news is God is ready to help us realize perfect peace and happiness if we will give Him control.

When considering a battle with a person or a group ask yourself these three questions first:

1. Does this person/group align with my beliefs?
2. Does this person/group serve me, and can I bring something to the group?
3. Do I want to be with this person/group?

If you answer no to any of these three questions, do not engage in the skirmish. Wait to confront this issue another day in another way. Waiting to respond may give you the answer to either walk away, let it be, or find a new approach.

If you are being accused of something, ask yourself: Are they right? If so, there's no defense—confess it to God, then do whatever you have to do to make it right before the sun sets on the day. If you must apologize, then do it. If you need to make amends or restitution, get at it!

If you are being accused and you are not guilty, there is no reason to defend yourself. The accuser probably isn't interested in the truth. Let God fight this fight for you—the truth will prevail, and you may get the opportunity to allow your polished armor to shine with them or someone else.

When it comes to spiritual war, gird yourself, protect your heart and quote to yourself:

The devil whispered in my ear,
"You're not strong enough to withstand the storm."
I smiled, raised my armor, and said,
"I am the storm!"

Pick Up Your Sword:

1. *"Love is patient, love is kind. It does not envy, it does not boast, it is not proud. It does not dishonor others, it is not self-seeking, it is not easily angered, it keeps no record of wrongs." ~1 Corinthians 13:4-5*
   What does this verse say about selfishness, control, and pride?

   _____

   _____

2. *"Do nothing out of selfish ambition or vain conceit. Rather in humility value others above yourselves" ~ Philippians 2:3 (NIV)*
   How shall we handle warfare according to this verse?

   _____

   _____

3. *"As for me and my house we will serve the Lord." ~Joshua 24:15 (NIV)*
   When trouble comes your way who will you be serving? What are you doing to be certain of your choice?

   _____

   _____

4. *"No one should seek their own good, but the good of others." ~ 1Corinthians 10:24 (NIV)*
   What does this verse mean? Should you stop self-care? Are there limits to seeking the good of others?

   _____

   _____

5. *"For by the grace given to me, I say to every one of you; Do not think of yourself more highly than you ought, but rather think of yourself with sober judgment, in accordance with the faith God has given each of you." ~Romans 12:3*
   Your thoughts:

   _____

   _____

Julia Ward Howe (1819-1910).

http://www.juliawardhowe.org/bio.htm

Howe was a poet and author, her most famous work being "The Battle Hymn of the Republic." She was also a social activist for women's suffrage.

Lesson 11

Safe Dreams and Dangerous Prayers

I can do all things through Him who strengthens me.
~Philippians 4:13

Hannah's story-

1 Samuel 1

Hannah was the primary wife to Elkanah. He had two wives: Hannah and Penimah. Pehimah had blessed Elkanah with children, but Hannah had not. In their culture, a woman's value was based on their ability to bear a male child. Penimah was merciless when the women went to the temple, she would make fun of Hannah.

One day Elkanah found Hannah crying and asked why. He was offended by her response of wanting a male child and replied, "Aren't I worth more than ten sons?"

Hannah at the temple fervently prayed for a child. The priest seeing her lips moving and her distraught manner asked if she was drunk and scolded her. She explained she was broken in spirit and had been praying to God for a child.

The Lord heard Hannah's prayers and blessed her with a son. She named him Samuel and committed him to the Lord's service. He became a prophet, leading the Israelites to victory over the Philistines ensuing a long period of peace.

Hannah inspires us to embrace our own power of prayer, trusting God's grace, provision, and blessings.

Praying Dangerous Prayers

Dreams stay elusive when we lock them away. Safe behind locked doors requests won't risk failure, and no one can criticize or challenge our dreams.

Staying in our comfort zone means just that, we will remain comfortable. It's familiar. In this space, there is no anxiety and no risk. We do not have to be vulnerable, and we can continue to pretend we are in control. The downside is that our dreams stay dreams without a chance of becoming a reality.

But if for a moment we move away from our 'safe' place and risk failing, feeling unsettled, or vulnerable, we may breathe the breath of life into our dreams and open entirely different opportunities. Opening the door is the starting point.

Pray. If you cannot pray about something or don't want to pray, try asking, "God make me want to want this."

Pray arrow prayers. Don't have time to pray? God doesn't care if you spend 10 seconds or 10 hours talking to Him. He delights in bringing all our concerns and requests to Him. Arrow prayers are short, sweet, in the moment prayers. They're quick but just as effective as long lengthy requests. I often pray over Facebook requests right then by saying, "Lord, I don't know all their needs, please hold them in your righteous right hand and answer their request." Simply including God in our daily needs is more important to Him than the length of the prayer.

Rewrite Scripture: Another tip for praying when you don't know what to say is to rewrite scripture using the person's name.

For example: Philippians 1:3-6

"³ I thank my God in all my remembrance of you, ⁴ always offering prayer with joy in my every prayer for you all, ⁵ in view of your participation in the gospel from the first day until now. ⁶ For I am confident of this very thing, that He who began a good work among you will complete it by the day of Christ Jesus."

Rewrite it like this:

³ I thank my God in all my remembrance of Karen, ⁴ always offering prayer with joy in my every prayer for Karen, ⁵ in view of your participation in the gospel from the first day until now. ⁶ For I am confident of this very thing, that He who began a good work in Karen will complete it by the day of Christ Jesus.

Pick Up Your Sword:

1. **The 'What if' game**: think of your scariest thoughts and write them down. Then one by one, ask what if I do this? What's the worst that could happen? For instance, if you are afraid to fail. Ask yourself, "What if I fail?" Then plan out that scenario. Going down that path can help you see that either your fear is senseless, or you'll know to plan better.

    _____

    _____

    _____

2. **What if I succeed game?** Write down what success could look like. Follow each idea until you reach the best-case scenario. Decide if that's what you really wanted when you started out. Do your research. Ask someone who has already found success. Then weigh your options and get moving.

_____

_____

_____

3. What if you ask God to build your faith and to trust him for the outcome? What might happen? Too often we don't include God in our plans. He said to ask. I believe He sits with us daily wanting to hand us a life of abundance, yet we don't ask. Ask!

_____

_____

_____

4. What dream have you dreamed but haven't pursued?

_____

_____

5. Why? What's stopping you?

_____

_____

(I'd rather be an old lady rocking on my front porch reliving the failures and the successes with no regrets than a woman who wonders what might have happened if I'd tried.)

6. *"Ask and it will be given to you; seek and you will find; knock and the door will be opened to you." ~ Matthew 7:7*
What does Matthew 7:7 say about asking in prayer for things?

_____

_____

7. God wants to show us who he is so I believe He waits until what we're asking for can only be answered by Him to demonstrate His love for us. *"The thief comes only to steal and kill and destroy; I came that they may have life and have it abundantly." ~ John 10:10*
What does John 10:10 promise us?

_____

_____

Harriet Jacobs (1813-1897).

https://en.wikipedia.org/wiki/Harriet_Ann_Jacobs

Jacobs, a writer, escaped slavery and later was freed. She published a novel, "Incidents in the Life of a Slave Girl," credited as the first to highlight the struggles of rape and sexual abuse within slavery.

The Power of Dangerous Prayers

> *Truly I tell you, if you have faith as small as a mustard seed,*
> *you can say to this mountain, 'Move from here to there,'*
> *and it will move.*
> *Nothing will be impossible for you."*
> *~Matthew 17:20*

Designed by our maker to be passionate, powerful women, why would we settle for mediocre or safe lives? We were not created for a life of comfort but are designed to be world changers, warriors, leaders, and teachers.

The Badass women of the Bible prayed for all kinds of things: to conceive babies, for food and shelter, to win battles, escape enemies and to discern truths.

They were bold, vulnerable, understood their strengths and who to align themselves with. They were often broken-hearted, and prayed in whispers, sobs or demands. Faith taught them they couldn't do everything, but they knew who could.

Be careful not to let our prayers be repetitive, dull, boring, rote, or thoughtless. That's like praying in a rut. Do you want more? It's time to pray, "Lord, change me into the kind of woman that could change the world. The kind that history or the world will remember because of good. The kind that if the Bible were written today, I would be included in it."

Let's start praying life changing, daring warrior leadership prayers that transform lives, communities and families.

Be aware though, when you pray daring prayers, you may experience desert times, attacks, trials, pain, and hardships. When you take a bold step out for Christ, you become an enemy to the enemy. You put a target on your back, but we know who has the power to win the battles! When you pray safe prayers, you are no threat to the enemy. Badass prayers bring about change that runs counter to the enemy's plans and glorifies God's. They inspire others to put on armor and fight too. When you pray setting an example, not only will you change, but the crowd of witnesses may just stop watching and pick up their swords to fight.

Pick Up Your Sword:

1. *"Come boldly to the throne of God." ~ Hebrew 4:16*
    What are we told we can do with our requests?

    _____

    _____

    _____

2. *"For I know the plans I have for you," declares the Lord, "plans to prosper you and not to harm you, plans to give you hope and a future." ~ Jeremiah 29:11*
    What does God want for us in Jeremiah 29:11?

    _____

    _____

    _____

3. *"Ask, and it will be given to you; seek, and you will find; knock and the door will be opened to you." ~ Matthew 7:7*
    What does God's word in Matthew 7:7 promise us?

    _____

    _____

    _____

4. Based on this lesson, how will you add or change what you are doing with prayer?

    _____

    _____

    _____

[Barbara Jordan](https://www.biography.com/people/barbara-jordan-9357991) **(1936-1996)**.

https://www.biography.com/people/barbara-jordan-9357991

Jordan was a lawyer, educator, politician, and civil rights movement leader. She was the first southern African American woman elected to the U.S. House of Representatives and the first African American woman to give a keynote address at the Democratic National Convention.

Prayer 101 – How to

> *"Prayer is not asking. It is a longing of the soul.*
> *It is daily admission of one's weakness.*
> *It is better in prayer to have a heart with no words*
> *than words without a heart."*
> *~Mahatma Gandhi*

The Widow's story: 2 Kings 4:1-7

A widow approached Elisha sharing her husband's death and that her unpaid debts left her unable to feed her sons or pay her bills. The bill collectors threatened to take her two sons and use them as slaves until the debt was paid in full.

Elisha asked what she had left in the house. She replied, "Nothing, except a small jar partially filled with oil." He told her to go borrow containers from all her neighbors, then to take her sons, close her doors, and pour from her little jar into all the containers she had gathered until they were full. She filled every container to the top. He told her to go sell the oil to pay her bills and she and her sons could live on the rest.

This story serves as a reminder of what we have learned, "We have not because we ask not; ask and it will be given." I understand our often reluctance to ask. I'm a really good giver but not so good at receiving from others. Perhaps I am too proud or simply like the role of giver better. But the action of prayer often begins with our asking for our needs. Asking forces us to acknowledge our need for help and who can meet that need. It builds dependency and relationships. The more we lean into this intimate relationship, the more we learn God delights to redeem, restore, refill, and replenish us.

If you are unsure how to pray try this simple acrostic A.C.T.S. until you develop your own style.

A = Appreciation. Acknowledge the greatness of God. (Sometimes I pray a worship song to Him.)

C = Confession. Admit the things you are doing wrong. Ask for forgiveness and commit to doing better. (This is NOT a salvation issue; this is an obedience issue.)

T = Thanksgiving. Thank God for all the things He has already done for you.

S = Supplication. Ask for your needs to be met. Ask for the needs of others. Pray His will, His scriptures back to him for your needs and requests. ("You said, I have not because I ask not, so I'm asking.")

And commit your prayer to His will. (I ask these things seeking Your will, not mine.)

Another prayer idea:

When it comes to praying for others, take the request very seriously. Keep a 3x5 card or a prayer journal with each person's name, the date, and the request. Pray daily for them. Ask for the need and for God to grant the request. Sometimes when I have a lot of requests, I send up arrow prayers with the cards while I am on the treadmill. Arrow prayers are single sentence (or two) simple quick prayers.

Cards also serve as a reminder to ask the person if and how the request was answered. It will also help you to see that God is still in the business of answering prayers. When the request is granted, write it down on the card with the date. Having a record of prayers and answers is a wonderful boost to the soul when we feel like the world is not going our way.

We have an Advocate, the Holy Spirit, so when we cannot find the words to pray the Holy Spirit will turn our silence or utterings into prayers that whisper in God's ear. I have experienced this type of prayer. I was so distraught over a situation that had, as far as I could see, no good outcome. The words would not come. I felt in my heart the utterings of the Holy Spirit within me and knew He was interceding for me. In a situation that was anything but peaceful, I experienced the "peace that passes all understanding." It came from some place deep within myself and I knew things would be alright.

Try praying A.C.T.S below. Write it down. As you use this technique, it won't always be necessary to write prayers down, but it is delightful to look back on a prayer journal to see later what you asked for and how it was answered.

A =_____

_____

_____

C = _____

_____

_____

T =_____

_____

_____

S =_____

_____

_____

"Prayer is not asking.
Prayer is putting oneself in the hands of God,
at His disposition,
and listening to His voice in the depth of our hearts."
~ Mother Teresa

Down through the ages, prayer has been twisted, formulated, and regulated. Do not make this mistake. Prayer is a conversation with a God that delights in every moment we spend with Him. Tell Him what's going on, and what you think. He already knows it, but He wants to share in our process, hopes, dreams, pain, and needs. Pray with a simple heart, vulnerable and authentic.

Pray with Simplicity:

1.   *"And when you come before God, don't turn that into a theatrical production either. All these people making a regular show out of their prayers, hoping for fifteen minutes of fame! Do you think God sits in a box seat?*
     ⁶ Here's what I want you to do: Find a quiet, secluded place so you won't be tempted to role-play before God. Just be there as simply and honestly as you can manage. The focus will shift from you to God, and you will begin to sense his grace." ~ Matthew 6:5-6 (The Message- MSG)
     What should we do and not do when we pray according to Matthew 6:5-8?

     _____

     _____

     _____

2.   *"I know your deeds, that you are neither cold nor hot; I wish that you were cold or hot. So, because you are lukewarm, and neither hot nor cold, I will spit you out of my mouth." ~ Revelation 3:15-16*
     What does Scripture warn about mediocre prayers in Revelation 3:15-16?

     _____

     _____

     _____

3.   "The world is full of so-called prayer warriors who are prayer-ignorant. They're full of formulas and programs and advice, peddling techniques for getting what they want from God. Don't fall for that nonsense. This is your Father you are dealing with, and he knows better than you what you need. With a God like this loving you, you can pray very simply. Like this:

     "Our Father in heaven, Reveal who you are.

Set the world right; Do what's best as above, so below.
Keep us alive with three square meals.
Keep us forgiven with you and forgiving others.
Keep us safe from ourselves and the Devil. You're in charge!
You can do anything you want! You're ablaze in beauty! Yes! Yes. Yes!"
~ Matthew 6:7-13 (The Message)
What should our prayers sound like?

_____

_____

_____

4. *"Teach me to do your will, for you are my God." ~ Psalm 143:10*
How will we become teachable to God's will?

_____

_____

_____

<u>Coretta Scott King</u> **(1927-2006)**.

https://www.biography.com/people/coretta-scott-king-9542067

The wife, and later widow, of Martin Luther King Jr. played an important role in preserving the legacy of the civil rights leader. Following his assassination in 1968, she founded the Martin Luther King Jr. Center for Nonviolent Social Change. She later lobbied for her late husband's birthday to be recognized as a federal holiday.

If God Already Knows then why pray?

If you then, being evil, know how to give good gifts to your children,
how much more will your Father, who is in heaven,
give what is good to those who ask Him!
~Matthew 7:11

Tabitha Acts 9:32-42

Tabitha was a disciple in the city of Jobba (you might know her as Dorcas—her Greek name.) Her life overflowed with kindness, loving acts, and caring for the needy. She worked hard to hand-sew clothing for the needy. She worked so hard she became sick and died.

Peter was touring the region and visited the people of Lydda. He healed a paralyzed man that had been confined to his bed for eight years. Everyone who lived in Lydda saw what had happened and began to worship the Lord.

Family and friends of Tabitha went about the job of washing her body and laid her in an upstairs room. Since Lydda was close to Jobba and when the disciples heard Paul was near, they sent for him saying, "Please come right away!"

When Peter arrived, they took him to the upper room. Widows, sobbing, showed him all the clothing Tabitha had made for others. They told tales of her kindness and generosity.

He sent everyone out of the room. He knelt and prayed. After a time, he said, "Tabitha, get up!" Then took her by her hand and led her out to her people. The news spread throughout Joppa and many committed their hearts to the Lord.

Why Pray?

If there ever was a reason to pray, it was at Tabitha's death. She was kind and motivated her community to go to bat for her. Prayer brought her back to life. Isn't our God of today the same God of Tabitha's generation? He hasn't changed. We learned in other Lesson s we don't have answers to prayer because we often don't ask for the specifics God can answer.

Prayer aligns us with God as we build a more intimate relationship with him. Time with God changes us. When we spend time with God in prayer, we build a bridge of communication that benefits us. When we pray over the little things, we become more prepared for the big things that come our way. And finally, our heavenly Father is ALWAYS there and available to listen and guide us.

We're told to ask for His will in our lives, for Him to return, for His will here on earth like in heaven, for our daily nutritional needs, to help us lead an honorable life and to protect us from the evils of the world.

Prayer demonstrates that we need God. It builds a relationship with Him. Prayer helps us understand who God is and teaches us to listen to Him for answers and who better to know what we need then the One who created us?

Prayer makes a difference. Throughout Scripture we see God's people pray and God answering those prayers. Think of Moses pleading with God to spare the Israelites from God's wrath after they had committed idolatry with the golden calf. God relented and had mercy on his people (Exodus 32:11-14). Or when Elijah asked God to send rain upon Israel after a long drought, and God sent a great rain (1 Kings 18:42-46). James tells us that "the prayer of a righteous person has great power as it is working." (James 5:16). When the Canaanite woman asked Jesus to heal her daughter. Jesus healed the blind and raised from the dead.

God wants to show us who He is, so I believe He waits until the answer can only be from Him to demonstrate His love for us. I guess the real question is "Why Not pray?" The benefits far outweigh the cost.

Prayer creates these things within us when done regularly:

- Eliminates worry and anxiety.

- Produces confidence to know we are loved and can approach the Lord and peace that assures me God is on the job even while I sleep.

- Gives direction to our lives and solutions to our problems.

- Sharpens discernment.

- Lifts our spirits and build joy.

- Protects us from trouble.

- Invites God into our daily lives, activities, and decisions.

- We receive answers to prayers! Miracles still happen!

- Prayer increases trust.

- Prayer offsets the negative health effects of stress.

- Prayer connects people who pray together.

- Prayer is the safe place where we can say things that no one else will ever understand.

- Prayer softens and humbles our heart.

Pick Up Your Sword:

1. *"Be anxious for nothing, but in everything by prayer and supplication with thanksgiving let your requests be made known to God. And the peace of God, which surpasses all comprehension, will guard your hearts and your minds in Christ Jesus."* ~ *Philippians 4:6-7*
    What does Philippians 4:6 say about the benefits of prayer?

    _____

    _____

    _____

2. *"The Lord said to him, "I have heard your prayer and your supplication, which you have made before Me; I have consecrated this house which you have built by putting My name there forever, and My eyes and My heart will be there perpetually."* ~ *1Kings 9:3*
    What will God do for us when we pray according to 1Kings 9:3?

    _____

    _____

    _____

<u>Dolley Madison</u> **(1768-1849).**

http://www.firstladies.org/biographies/firstladies.aspx?biography=4

Madison was the nation's first lady during James Madison's presidency from 1809-1817. She helped to furnish the newly reconstructed White House in 1814, after the invading British burned it to the ground, and is credited with saving the Lansdowne portrait of George Washington from the flames.

Lesson 15

The Value of a Good Argument

"Ask for what you want and be prepared to get it!"
~Maya Angelou

The Canaanite Woman

Her Story – Matthew 15:21-31

A Canaanite woman hunting down Jesus in the district of Tyre and Sidon cried out to him saying, "Have mercy on me, Lord, my daughter is demon possessed." Jesus did not answer her. She followed Him and the disciples and continued to ask for her daughter's healing. The disciples grew weary and begged Him to send her away. He answered and said, "I was sent only to the lost sheep of the house of Israel."

The woman bowed down to Jesus and begged, "Lord, help me!" Jesus answered her, "It's not good to take the children's bread and throw it to the dogs." She argued, "Yes, Lord; but even the dogs feed on the crumbs which fall from their masters' table."

Impressed, Jesus said to her, "Woman, your faith is great it shall be done for you as you wish." And her daughter was healed immediately.

The Bible does not tell us the woman's name and we hear nothing else about her. It makes me wonder why this story was included in the scriptures. Perhaps we are reminded to ask for our needs. And her request was granted due to her great faith in Christ's ability to do what she was asking. Do we? Do we have enough moxie to persistently hound Christ for the desires of our hearts?

What can we learn from this woman? Perhaps it's time to believe we have a source of power that can answer impossible prayers. We need to learn to ask for what we need expecting results. She wouldn't take no for an answer. If our hearts are in the pathway of righteousness and we're asking with a right motive, why can't we ask for the unconceivable prayers? Scripture tells us we can. Why don't we?

Pick Up Your Sword:

1. *"Rejoice always, pray without ceasing, give thanks in all circumstances; for this is the will of God in Christ Jesus for you." ~ 1 Thessalonians 5:16-18*
   Your thoughts:

   _____

   _____

   _____

2. *"This is the confidence we have in approaching God: that if we ask anything according to his will, he hears us." ~ 1 John 5:14*
   Your thoughts:

   _____

   _____

   _____

3. *"Therefore, I tell you, whatever you ask for in prayers, believe that you have received it, and it will be yours." ~ Mark 11:24*
   Your thoughts:

   _____

   _____

   _____

4. *"The Lord is near to all who call on him, to all who call on him in truth." ~ Psalm 145:18*
   Your thoughts:

   _____

   _____

   _____

5. *"If you, then though you are evil, know how to give good gifts to your children, how much more will your Father in heaven give good gifts to those who ask him!" ~ Matthew 7:11*
   Your thoughts:

   _____

   _____

   _____

<u>Sandra Day O'Connor</u> **(1930-2020).**

https://www.biography.com/people/sandra-day-oconnor-9426834

A lawyer, O'Connor became a celebrated judge and eventually the first female justice on the Supreme Court, serving from 1981-2006. President Ronald Reagan appointed her.

Emotionally Healthy or Faking it?

"Stepping onto a brand-new path is difficult,
but not more difficult than remaining in a situation,
which is not nurturing to the whole woman."
~ Maya Angelou

Ever feel like a circus clown juggling too many balls in the air? Unmanaged time can feel like we are on a merry-go-round that is spinning out of control. Fatigue sets in and the chaos increases. This season of unrest can be brought on by our lack of time management, people pleasing desires, grief, new situations, and over-commitment.

But with a few small steps, there are things we can do to cope.

Care for your creative side

Get involved in a DIY (do it yourself) project. Sew Placemats, upholster a chair, paint an end table, cook from scratch, and try something new.

Care for your mental and emotional side

Form a new support group around your own superpower. If you're excellent at couponing, form a group that's like-minded and teach or share it.

Do something out of your comfort zone. Attend a book reading, a cooking class, a political group, animal shelter or load a new app and play it with a friend like, geocaching, scrabble, or Trivial Pursuit.

Care for your spiritual side

Join a prayer group or form one of your own. Join a support group or engage a counselor. Seek out a life coach. Try meditation of Tai Chi, or Yoga, walk, swim, hike and develop your powers of observation.

Care for your intellectual side

Take a class designed to stretch you. Take in a lecture on a topic you know nothing about but are interested in. Attend podcasts, webinars, and audio books on interesting subjects. Read a book.

TURN OFF:

FOMO — Fear of Missing Out. We're often so afraid that we'll miss out on something that we allow too many distractions. Put away the fear that you don't already have enough and enjoy being present.

TV — I remember when there were three available channels: ABC, NBC, and CBS. Today there are over 400 channels. Although there are a few valuable shows, most of them are time wasters. If you can't go without, record them and watch them while you do laundry, dishes or walk on the treadmill.

Social Media — Facebook, Twitter, Instagram, and 15 more before I end this sentence, all designed to vie for our attention. Build personal boundaries around them, limit the opportunities to slide down that endless rabbit hole stealing hours of our lives we can't get back and may produce nothing beneficial. Limit.

Negative people and takers — Some people are only in our lives for a season, when that season passes if they aren't a positive influence in our life, let them go.

TURN ON:

Mindful thinking — Practice being aware daily, minute by minute. Life's opportunities arrive but we must be present and available to notice.

Positive people and their positive thinking — Glean from them how they stay positive and what they think about and focus on. Seek out people in your area of dreams, and then find those that are further along the path than you are and ask them to help you.

Healthy life choices — Give up old habits that aren't producing forward motion for life choices. Fight for you. Then develop good choices and try to incorporate them daily. Self-care is anything we do to intentionally prioritize our health mentally, physically, emotionally, and spiritually. We can be stewards of our temple loaned to us by Christ by walking in our purpose, building our relationship with Christ by reading and praying. Self-care means that we see our health (physically and emotionally) as a gift that we must care for intentionally. When we care for ourselves, we are able to live out our purpose and care for others.

Tips for Self-Care:

- Journal

- Memorize verses.

- Write verses out on note cards.

- Pray through them.

- Find an accountability/prayer partner.

- Make a play list of praise songs.

Pick Up Your Sword:

1. *"Don't you know that you are God's temple and that God's Spirit dwells in your midst?"* ~ 1Corinthians 3:16
Your thoughts:

_____

_____

_____

2. *"Do not be conformed to this world but be transformed by the renewing of your mind. Then you will be able to test and approve what God's will is—his good, pleasing, and perfect will."* ~ Romans 12:2
Your thoughts:

_____

_____

_____

3. *"I can do all things through Christ who strengthens me."* ~ Philippians 4:13
Your thoughts:

_____

_____

_____

4. *"Do you not know that your bodies are temples of the Holy Spirit, who is in you, whom you have received from God? You are not your own; you were bought at a price. Therefore, honor God with your bodies."* ~ 1Corinthians 6:19-20
Your thoughts:

_____

_____

_____

5. *"A cheerful heart is good medicine, but a crushed spirit dries up the bones."* ~ Proverbs 17:22
Your thoughts:

_____

_____

_____

6. *"The Lord will guide you always; He will satisfy your needs in a sun-scorched land and will strengthen your frame. You will be like a well-watered garden, like a spring whose waters never fail."* ~ Isaiah 58:11
Your thoughts:

_____

_____

Rosa Parks (1913-2005).

Parks was the most prominent female face of the civil rights movement. In December 1955, Parks refused to give up her seat in the "colored section" of a bus to a white man and was charged with civil disobedience. She is known as "the mother of the freedom movement."

Feelings or Anxiety?

"Almost everything will work again
if you unplug it for a few minutes,
Including you. "
~Anne Lamott

Webster defines feelings as an emotional state or a reaction to something. Emotions can be a vague or an irrational feeling. When we allow emotions to dictate, they can hi-jack good intentions.

Our day-to-day lives are filled with good and bad feelings. It is what we do with our emotional state of mind that determines their worth. Feelings can be much like a rut in the road, they are familiar. Try as we might, we tend to end up in the rut unless we define the emotions and the solutions.

Define your feelings: Take a moment to feel what you are feeling. Take a deep breath and focus on what is going on. First eliminate being hungry or tired. These two body reactions can be interpreted as feelings and show up as frustration, anxiety, being sick, unhappy or being overwhelmed.

If you are hungry—eat. If you are tired, delay dealing with decisions until you can sleep. The saying 'sleep on it' was never more important than now.

There is another old saying, "If you can name it, you can tame it." Try to get to the origin of the problem. Spend the time being able to recognize the real feeling before having a knee-jerk reaction.

No more laters: Often our emotions can pile up on us because we don't know what to do with what we're feeling, or we put off saying or doing what we already know we should do. By avoiding dealing with situations, we grow them like weeds. Write down what you are feeling, search for the cause, and address it. If you make the wrong choice, go back, and change it, but do not let it sit and simmer. If you need to address something with a person, do it. Word it carefully, and then trust them to be part of the solution.

Write it down: Feelings left inside our hearts and minds tend to fester and grow far beyond the original cause. Writing them down forces us to clarify what the feeling is and its value to us. Often seeing it in black and white removes the power or at least lessens the influence it has over us.

Buffer thoughts and actions: Reacting to emotions rarely creates the outcome you are hoping for. Take a moment away from the emotion, take several deep, slow breaths and clarify your thoughts, then say what you are thinking to yourself before speaking it aloud. This simple exercise can help you respond rather than react.

Control your thoughts rather than allowing thoughts to control you: Thoughts, feelings, moods, only have power if you let them. We can get in the habit of allowing thoughts to govern us so often that it's like running a train down the tracks at 100 miles per hour by the caboose. The caboose is important to the train but is not equipped to run the engine.

Not every emotion needs a platform: Giving a voice to every emotion that swims past our awareness can be exhausting. Acknowledging a feeling and giving it a nod to continue past our stream of consciousness allows emotions that should be dealt with the energy to do so.

Watch your mouth: Negative emotions are a part of human nature, talking about them doesn't have to be. Take a moment to understand why you have the negative emotion come up with a positive way to handle it and speak the solution. If you always say, "I'm fat, or I'm always going to be broke" you will be. I remember as a child someone telling me, "If you focus on having a fire-breathing dragon long enough, you will have one." What they were warning me about was where your mind spends its time, is the world you will create. Speak positively as often as you can. Be the person in the room that fills it with positive energy rather than one that sucks the room dry.

Be aware of the mountains and valleys For every mountain top emotion, there will be an equal low. Your world did not fall apart. The dip is the mind's way of bringing you back to your homeostasis or base line. It takes great energy to be on an upward run, so build into your surges times of rest. Practice regular pauses to renew your energy and thinking. Put your breaks on your calendar until they become second nature.

View the forest, not just the trees: Life up close is vital for a mindful awareness, but it is equally important to take a step back. The view from a distance will afford new perspectives on your life/work balance and goals.

I am not suggesting we stop our emotions, but I am suggesting we recognize them rather than thinking they are the headliners in every story. We should feel emotional, we are wired to be sensitive. There will be days when the world feels like it is on tilt; note it, plan accordingly and define the feelings when we are not standing on the edge of a cliff.

We all experience difficult emotions like pain, sorrow, sadness, anger, etc. Sometimes negative emotions knock us out of complacency. Being uncomfortable may wake us up to negative situations and propel positive change. Defining the emotions can afford us the ability to use them for good.

Choose different words in the sentences in your head. If you cannot talk nice about yourself, then quote affirmative Bible verses until the negative tone finds a positive meter.

If you can, define how you feel about things before you share them with others to avoid being heavily influenced. Protect your own instincts and feelings. There will be times you will need outside counsel—use it. There is no shame in collecting resources and others' ideas, especially if they have already walked where you are attempting to go. When you have decided how you feel by giving yourself enough time to think, then create the solution.

Pick Up Your Sword:

1. Take ten minutes every day to just sit with your thoughts. Try listing them and then numbering them in priority and start working on the most important one. What are your top three feelings or situations that might cause you stress or anxiety?

    a. _____
    b. _____
    c. _____

2. What are your ways of handling anxiety? Name 3. (if you can't name 3 ways, it's time to be a better steward of you and research ideas)

    a. _____
    b. _____
    c. _____

3. *"Cast all your anxieties on him because he cares for you." ~ 1 Peter 5:7*
    Your thoughts:

    _____
    _____
    _____

4. *"For God gave us a spirit not of fear but of power and love and self-control."*
    ~ 2 Timothy 1:7 (ESV)
    Your thoughts:

    _____
    _____
    _____

5. So, we can confidently say, *"The Lord is my helper; I will not fear; what can man do to me?" ~ Hebrews 13:6 (ESV)*
    Your thoughts:

    _____
    _____
    _____

6. *"Anxiety in a man's heart weighs him down, but a good word makes him glad."* ~ *Proverbs 12:25 (ESV)*
   Your thoughts:

   _____

   _____

   _____

7. *"Fear not, for I am with you; be not dismayed, for I am your God; I will strengthen you, I will help you, I will uphold you with my righteous right hand."* ~ *Isaiah 41:10*
   Your thoughts:

   _____

   _____

   _____

<u>Sally Ride</u> **(1951-2012)**.

https://www.space.com/16756-sally-ride-biography.html

A physicist and astronaut, Ride joined NASA in 1978. Five years later, in 1983, she became the first American woman to go to outer space.

Define Your Internal Dialogue

> One evening, an elderly Cherokee brave told his
> grandson about a battle that goes on inside people.
> He said "My son, the battle is between two 'wolves' inside us all.
> One is evil. It is anger, envy, jealousy, sorrow,
> regret, greed, arrogance, self-pity, guilt, resentment,
> inferiority, lies, false pride, superiority, and ego.
> The other is good. It is joy, peace love, hope serenity,
> humility, kindness, benevolence, empathy, generosity,
> truth, compassion and faith."
> The grandson thought about it for a minute and then asked his grandfather:
> "Which wolf wins?"
> The old Cherokee simply replied, "The one that you feed."

You are intentionally knit together for a purpose. You are uniquely and wonderfully made. You need to respect that design. If not, what do you tell yourself about who you are and why you're here?

If we believe we were created to fill a void in the world that only we can fill, then our internal dialogue should equal that calling.

Most of us spend far more time worrying, or talking to ourselves in such negative ways, or worried about what others will think. We take up too much heart and brain space in a state of angst that could be used for filling our destinies.

I once heard a speaker say, "If you were in a coma, and woke up one day minus your memory but with all other faculties, and the people around you told you that you were a Navy Seal and the Navy wants you back; think how differently you would talk to yourself and behave than if when you woke up you were told you were a drug addict that overdosed?"

Discovering who we are, what we're passionate about, and what our why is in life, helps determine our next steps. Once we find what gives our life meaning and purpose it puts us in charge of the direction of our life. Whatever our life's work is, let's start moving towards it. What is one step you can take today toward your goal?

If you don't know your purpose, ask yourself why am I still here? Take the spiritual gifting test and begin to make conscious efforts to find and move toward the goal of being all you can be. Your life is worth finding. It may not happen all at once or overnight, but it can start a little every day. Be willing to explore the opportunities that present themselves. Prospects are embraceable if we are prepared for them. We may need to get up earlier, run a bit faster, learn a new skill, end a bad habit, stretch ourselves and be willing to be uncomfortable.

Fear kills dreams, hopes, relationships, and holds us paralyzed.

Fear is a state of mind that can be changed. Self-esteem is a state of being satisfied with yourself. If you are not satisfied, then believe better and do better.

How do we get started changing the way we talk to ourselves?

1. Start listing the things you like about yourself.

2. Be present. Turn off distractions and notice how well you do or don't handle things so you can embrace or change the direction.

3. Find a mentor(s). Or pay attention to someone you admire. Write down the things they do that you look up to or that you'd like to adopt into your own life.

4. Take your mentor to coffee. Ask them what they think their strengths and weaknesses are, and how their strengths became strong.

5. Ask your mentor what strengths and weaknesses they see in you and what advice they might have for your 'next step'.

6. Get rid of distractions and time wasters. Start reading, taking courses, listening to podcasts, speakers who have good advice for inspiring your best self.

7. Lose negative influences. Begin to filter what is detrimental. Build boundaries to protect your heart and mind.

8. Learn how to fight for what you want so you can hold your position.

9. Listen to criticism, the true stuff use, the unkind stuff—forget.

Expect challenges and criticisms and turn them into lessons.

What's the bottom line? Live your unique purpose.

Fight for you. Believe in you. Dare to be different!

Pick Up Your Sword:

1. List 10 things about yourself that you like and/or are strengths.

   _____

   _____

   _____

2. What distractions are robbing you of moving forward?

   _____

   _____

   _____

3. What strengths does your mentor have that you admire?

   _____

   _____

   _____

4. What strengths does your mentor say you have?

   _____

   _____

   _____

5. *"She opens her mouth in wisdom, and the teaching of kindness is on her tongue." ~ Proverbs 31:26*
   What can we learn from Proverbs 31:26?

   _____

   _____

   _____

6. What affirmations and powerful words can you say to yourself daily?

   _____

   _____

   _____

Sacagawea was a Lemhi Shoshone woman best known for her expedition with Lewis and Clark through the territory of the Louisiana Purchase. The Native American traveled from North Dakota to the Pacific Ocean with the explorers.

Rein and Measure Your Words

Wise men speak because they have something to say,
fools speak because they have to say something.
~ Plato

Have you ever been in a room where it's easy to pick out the confident people? It's just as easy to notice the people who have very little or low self-esteem. We tend to judge other people's confidence by their behaviors, their life choices, and how they speak.

The words we use tell others more about us than we think. How and when we use them might determine how others judge our personal confidence. There are no whistle-blowing referees to cut us off from using words that miss-align us when we talk.

You may recognize some of these confidence-sapping words:

Um and Ah – Whenever we find a temporary loss of words, rather than pausing slightly, to fill the space, we use "um" and "ah." Those who have made the decision to use these two crutch words may appear less confident or less educated. If you're used to filling every space in conversation, stop . . . , pause . . . , then restate. One of the training tools I use in my speech class is to videotape the person giving the talk. It helps them see what habits they repeat.

Always and Never – Rarely does anything "always" or "never" happen. Generalizing and using these words limits a discussion or are used to place the burden of the blame on someone in conversations. These two words can burn the bridge of communication that you might want to cross over. Find more accurate words.

Like and You Know – Some people can't talk without using the word "like" or the phrase "you know" as a connecting word or phrase to run all their sentences together. It's a habit we pick up when we're tweens, using it as an adult will flag you as immature. Instead pause before speaking to avoid gap fillers.

Just and what-not should be stricken from all written and spoken language. The words are modifiers and are rarely used correctly. I know someone who uses the word "just" to soften their requests, but all it does is weaken the appeal. Drop the word and say what you mean to say without modifying it.

Kinda, sorta, and whatever – These words aren't yes or no. They don't even really define the word maybe. Vagueness makes you look like you either have no backbone, don't know what you think, or are afraid to take a stand. These words make you look naïve and timid. Strike them from your vocabulary.

Sorry – Repeating "sorry" over and over when it isn't necessary or needed takes the power from a genuine "I'm sorry." It makes the word trite rather than meaningful. If you need to apologize to someone, say it in a way that makes them feel you mean it.

F-Bomb – I'm not fond of swearing, but am aware that an occasional well-placed curse word can bring weight to a point. But most times this one is overused and emphasizes nothing. As much as I don't like to judge, it often places the speaker on a less than classy, unsophisticated level. It also makes a listener question the person's level of education, robbing them of elegance and grace. Cut curse words from your conversations.

One of the characteristics of a woman worth admiring is a sense of mystery. Don't be a chatterbox, which makes a person look desperate, self-focused or afraid to hear her own thoughts. Instead, be slow to speak. I remember being in a group situation where one of the women only spoke up when she had some quality comment to add to the conversation, and I noticed the room quieted whenever she spoke up. I want to be that kind of influencer.

Making any change is tough, but these changes will allow the real you to be seen. Sometimes weak speaking habits can keep people from hearing you as a person. You can be judged too quickly and written off before you really get a chance. My father used to tell me, "It's better to be thought a fool than to open your mouth unbecomingly and remove all doubt."

Strong, confident women know there is power in words. Here are some words strung together in such a way as to inspire us:

Pick Up Your Sword:

1. What weak speaking habits do you need to get rid of?

    _____

    _____

    _____

2. *"Let no corrupting talk come out of your mouths, but only such as is good for building up, as fits the occasion, that it may give grace to those who hear."*
    ~ Ephesians 4:29 (ESV)
    Your thoughts:

    _____

    _____

    _____

3. *"I tell you, on the day of judgment people will give account for every careless worth they speak..."* ~ *Matthew 12:36 (ESV)*
    Your thoughts:

    _____

    _____

    _____

4. *"Death and life are in the power of the tongue, and those who love it will eat its fruits."* ~ *Proverbs 18:21*
    Your thoughts:

    _____

    _____

    _____

5. *"A word fitly spoken is like apples of gold in a setting of silver."*
    ~ *Proverbs 25:11 (ESV)*
    Your thoughts:

    _____

    _____

    _____

6. *"Let your speech always be gracious, seasoned with salt, so that you may know how you ought to answer each person."* ~ *Colossians 4:6 (ESV)*
    Your thoughts:

    _____

    _____

    _____

<u>Phyllis Schlafly</u> **(1924-2016)**.

http://eagleforum.org/about/bio.html

Schlafly was a constitutional lawyer and conservative political activist. She is best known for her critiques of radical feminism and her successful campaign against ratification of the Equal Rights Amendment to the Constitution.

Does Your Confidence Propel or Sabotage You?

You gain strength, courage, and confidence by every experience
in which you really stop to look fear in the face.
You are able to say to yourself, 'I lived through this horror.
I can take the next thing that comes along.'
~ Eleanor Roosevelt

I am woman hear me roar, or are you gumming yourself through life? There are two kinds of confidence a person may embrace. One comes from a strong, quiet strength and the second type comes from a fear-based confidence.

Quiet confidence is an inner strength that does not have to be talked about or placed on a résumé; it shows in a person's demeanor. These are the people who do not have to shove their opinions down people's throats. They do not need to scream from the rooftops their ideas or beliefs; it is demonstrated in their day-to-day choices, how they handle situations, and how they manage stresses. When you spend time with these people, you walk away feeling as if you were the only person they came to see. They give energy because they have it to give. They inspire because they are inspired. They are the ones who can find joy in any situation, or at the very least they can turn a negative into a positive. Quiet confident people are on-purpose people. They have learned from the past and are moving forward. They have an attitude that says, "Been there; done that; I'll do it again." They operate from an offensive position.

One of the differences between confident women and those who lack confidence is experience. Once you have walked through tough situations, you have the knowledge to know how to deal with it, which breeds confidence for future similar events.

Things confident, strong women NEVER do:

- **Gossip**. They understand that dimming others' lights does not make their light shine brighter.
- **Judgmental**. They understand everyone has a story and even if it's not the best, they're quick to be equipping and inspiring.
- **Blame others**. No one wins at the blame shifting game.

- **Self-deprecating talk**. Words are powerful. Negative talk about yourself creates a downward esteem spiral. Bite your tongue, if you must, to avoid self-defeating words.

- **Control every situation**. The need to control every situation means the confidence is originating from a place of fear and is rarely positive.

- **They do not judge others**. They are comfortable enough to have room for a wide variety of people.

- **They are not attention seeking**. There is a difference between being outgoing, and enjoying life, and doing things that intentionally draw attention to themselves. They show genuine interest in others rather than talking about just themselves. They engage others in conversation.

- **Bragging is not their style**. If there's bragging to be done, they let others do it.

- **They are not drama queens**. They have learned not to over complicate things. Confident women act rationally and do not feel a need to run the show by their emotions.

- **Attitude down**. Confident women rarely project an attitude as their first line of communication. They can give birth to one when situations call for it, but they do not camp there.

- **Failure does not frighten them**. They understand that failing means you are trying, so they embrace the effort, fail, adjust and try again.

- **They do not break their word or find it necessary to lie**. They have assessed the situation, answer slowly, and then respond in order to avoid cover-ups or breaking their commitments.

- **Waste time**. Confident women understand the true cost of time and that people matter most. They spend their time wisely to place people at the top of their priority list.

- **They do not live in the past**. Strong women appreciate that there is nothing that can be done to change the past, and worry doesn't change anything, so they move forward.

- **Negative**. Confident women have learned to avoid negative people, places, and energy. They are aware that limit time in negative situations is the best way to protect themselves.

Things confident women do:

- **They understand and embrace their strengths and gifting**. They make a daily effort to place themselves in jobs, relationships and circumstances that utilize their specific aptitudes.

- **They make a point of assessing their weaknesses and seek out opportunities to build them into strengths**.

- **They cherish their friends and families**, but they make a point of spending time alone. They have learned how to be their own good company. There is value in entertaining yourself and being alone with your thoughts. We all need time when we are free of others' expectations and demands.

- **They accept their own body image**. It is one thing to be health conscious and to take care of yourself first in order to be there for others, but more importantly strong women know how to embrace their own uniqueness. There is more to worry about in life than hair color and thigh size.

- **They may be victims, but they do not stay there**. They actively pursue what it takes to move through the event. They do not give away their power.

- **They take time for themselves**. You cannot give away what you don't have yourself.

- **They embrace change**. Rather than complain that things are different, they look for the positive in the new adventure.

- **They do not waste time on things they can't control**. They accept the uncontrollable items and make a path around the obstacles.

- **They are kind and practice good manners**.

- **They work hard to have others feel important**.

Pick Up Your Sword:

1. *"If you don't like something, change it. If you can't change it, change your attitude." ~ Maya Angelou*
   What does this quote say to you?

   _____

   _____

   _____

2. What areas do you lack confidence in? Why?

   _____

   _____

   _____

3. *"A positive attitude gives you power over your circumstances instead of your circumstances having power over you." ~ Joyce Meyer*
   What does this quote say to you about your power?

   _____

   _____

   _____

4. *"A calm mind brings inner strength and self-confidence, so that's very important for good health." ~ Dalai Lama*
   What does this quote say to you about self-confidence?

   _____

   _____

   _____

5. *"For the Lord will be your confidence and will keep your foot from being caught." ~ Proverbs 3:26 (ESV)*
   What does this verse say to you?

   _____

   _____

   _____

6. *"In the fear of the Lord one has strong confidence, and his children will have a refuge." ~ Proverbs 14:26*
   What does this verse say where confidence starts?

   _____

   _____

   _____

7. *"Therefore, do not throw away your confidence, which has a great reward. For you have need of endurance, so that when you have done the will of God you may receive what is promised." ~ Hebrews 10:25 (ESV)*
Why should we build confidence according to Hebrews?

_____

_____

_____

The abolitionist and author's most well-known work is the novel "Uncle Tom's Cabin," which portrayed the impact of slavery on families and children. Its impact led to Stowe's meeting with President Abraham Lincoln.

Fear or Confidence-They can't exist together

> *"Be who you are and say what you feel,*
> *because those who mind don't matter,*
> *and those who matter don't mind."*
> *~Bernard M. Baruch*

Fear-based confidence operates from a defensive position—a bite-before-bitten attitude. This individual may look like they are in charge and can handle life or situations, but truthfully, they are scared. This type of confidence tends always to be announcing themselves—they are often the résumé flinger. They want you to know that they can handle a job. They often discuss past successes or may turn most conversations into glowing reports about them. They have a need for you to know how adept they are in a multitude of situations.

Here's the good and the bad of fear-based confidence for the individual and the people around them: they may feel it's necessary to always over-deliver, which will over time be exhausting. For instance, if they are giving 150% at work, they have little, or nothing left for other parts of their life. Short-changing their energy in the rest of their life will cause a tug-of-war lifestyle between relationships and work. When they recognize this imbalance, their desire to right it can lead then to throwing their energy into the relationship elements of their life, which leaves their work percentage out of line. They are out of balance.

The truth is we only have 100% effort to give. Not having it allocated properly is dissatisfying to us but as well as the people in our lives. The frustration for maintaining the re-allocation of our focus can drain our energy and joy for life.

What's the solution for a fear-based confidence?

1. **Take an inventory of your skills, talents, and strengths**. It might be a good lesson to humbly ask others you trust what they believe are your character strengths and abilities. Hearing what others think may help you to better understand your place in the world. It might also have the capacity to help you better understand your worth.

2. **Stop the negative thoughts and self-doubting**. This might be a tougher lesson, and you may need some professional guidance, but do it. We tend to have self-loathing or lack of personal recognition of our strengths and can be quick to see our shortcomings. There is strength in knowing who we are and

being comfortable with our real self. Without it, we can doom ourselves to a life that exists on a gerbil wheel.

3. **Assess your life.** your job, your living situation, and your relationships, and ask yourself why you have what you have. Are you accepting less than what is best for you? If so, change it. Be bold; change it. Life is too short to settle for mediocre. That might mean you have to work on your relationships by changing yourself or bringing new life to it with real communication. You might have to take steps to change your job or where you are living. You may be working a job that is either out of your personal gifting, lacks your passion or you are in over your head. Do not just continue because of inertia; evaluate and change. Your passion depends on clarity.

4. **Be vulnerable**. This step is tougher for fear-based individuals. It means you'll have to be open enough to put aside all the protection mechanisms you're used to using. Decide instead that you are enough, and this is an adventure to discover new territory within yourself. It won't be easy and will feel so awkward you'll be tempted to run back to what you know.

5. **Down shift**. Slow your life down in such a way that you have time to respond rather than to react. Fear-based confidence tends to react to situations too quickly. Do whatever you can to slow your life down to have time to think before answering or following through. Moving at the speed of light will keep you highly charged emotionally. This is neither useful for decision making, your immune system or living a peaceful life.

Confidence is an evolving maturity. Sometimes you may get to the quiet strength type of confidence because you have also reached the "I quit" point in your life. Sometimes when you have nothing to lose, you are better able to determine an enhanced life for yourself. However, the energy you will use to come to that point can have adverse health effects and cost you dearly in emotional health and/or relationships.

Pick Up Your Sword:

Tips for Building Confidence

Here are twenty tips to move you from lack of confidence to a comfortable, confident life. Which 5 can you start today?

1. Learn something new. Read a book, take a class, try something you never thought you would. It will empower you.

2. Do something for someone else. Take the focus off you; the feel-good-about-yourself enzymes you'll stir up can carry you to the next level.

3. Organize something. It does not have to be big; it might just be a junk drawer or vacuuming behind the couch. You'll know it. That is enough for now.

4. Build a bucket list and start checking things off. Hang it where you will see it daily. Plan to accomplish one of them a month.

5. Write a note of appreciation for someone that you know rarely gets thanked for their job.

6. Plan for success. Put your gym clothes on in the morning and place your shoes where you will trip on them first thing.

7. Keep a diary. Write down your thoughts. Writing has a way of helping you know what you know and bringing facts to emotional thoughts.

8. Step out of your comfort zone. If you are an introvert, go to a book signing, a networking group, or a particular fund-raising event. If you are an extrovert, practice sitting alone with yourself, book a hotel room alone with just your thoughts, or unplug from all electronic social media for days or—GASP—a week!

9. Work out. The movement will kick in the "I can accomplish anything" feel-good enzymes.

10. Never make decisions when you are in a vulnerable state. Make a Ben Franklin list, then walk away from it for a day or two.

11. Make a plan of things that matter to you and how you are going to acquire them.

12. Ask yourself who you are, what you stand for, what you will not tolerate. Then evaluate situations where you are allowing things you should not and do not do what you desire and change them.

13. When you are afraid of looking foolish, embrace the idea that if you knew how little others think about others, you could move through mistakes easier.

14. Break big projects that scare you into smaller pieces and just do the first step and then the next.

15. When it comes to fear holding you back, do whatever it is that scares you before you have a chance to talk yourself out of it.

16. Acknowledge your doubts, then train them or prepare better, then move forward anyway.

17. Ban the word "can't" from your vocabulary.

18. Stop people pleasing because you are afraid of _____ (you fill in the blank). Please people because you choose to, not because you think you must.

19. We all run our lives and values on self-created rules. Make your rules answer to your needs today. They may have been good ideas in the past but no longer serve you anymore.

20. Insert yourself into new experiences. Multi-faceted people have more understanding of who they are.

We may move from one type of confidence to the other depending on the seasons in our life we are experiencing. If you predominately operate from a defensive spirit, perhaps understanding why will move you to a confident offensive mindset. The "why" may not be immediately clear, so move forward by practicing one of the tips above until you can determine the "why." If nothing else works, build your bucket list, and hit the gym!

What are some things confident people do in your circle of influence that you can emulate?

_____

_____

_____

<u>Sojourner Truth</u> **(1797-1883).**

https://www.biography.com/people/sojourner-truth-9511284

An abolitionist and women's rights activist, Truth was born into slavery and escaped with her infant daughter to freedom in 1826. She became best known for her "Ain't I a Woman?" speech on racial inequalities in 1851 at the Ohio Women's Rights Convention.

Defining Courage

"Courage is not just one of the virtues
but the form of every virtue at the testing point."
~ C.S. Lewis

What exactly is courage? A feeling? An action? Looking tough?

Everyone is frightened of something. While we can't change an emotional response, we can change how we react to the fear.

Everyone wants to be courageous but what does that mean? There are as many types of courage as there are people. There's physical courage, mental courage, moral courage, and situational courage.

Physical Courage: Being afraid but choosing to act

Courage is a virtue, a habit, that you can develop. Habits are like a muscle. You can train them with experience. The more often we act courageous the easier the next situation requiring courage becomes.

One way to develop courage is to define how we feel about issues and situations before we are standing waist deep in the decision, then when we must decide on an issue we can't prepare for, our courage muscle will be skilled. Developing our courage on a regular basis might cause us to be influenced by others' opinions. We can make our decision, state it politely without the typical emotional intensity.

Emotional Courage: It starts in your heart

It is often easier to be courageous for the benefit of others. We need to know why and who we are being courageous for. Be present and note how you feel powerful when you stand up for others and seek that same strength for yourself. Steve Jobs in a Stanford commencement speech said, "And most important, have the courage to follow your heart and intuition. They somehow already know what you genuinely want to become. Everything else is secondary."

Mel Robbins reminds us that our brains are hardwired to protect us and if we do not have the courage to act on our instincts and ideas within five seconds, we won't move at all.

Greatness, great ideas live and die within our hearts and minds. Act on your courage today and there will be more tomorrow to draw on when life throws something our way that requires great courage.

Pick Up Your Sword:

1. *"It takes courage…to endure the sharp pains of self-discovery rather than choose to take the dull pain of unconsciousness that would last the rest of our lives." ~ Marianne Williamson*
    Your thoughts?

    _____
    _____
    _____

2. *"For God has not given us a spirit of fear, but of power and of love and of a sound mind." ~ 2 Timothy 1:7*
    Your thoughts:

    _____
    _____
    _____

3. *"Have I not commanded you? Be strong and courageous. Do not be frightened, and do not be dismayed, for the Lord your God is with you wherever you go." ~ Joshua 1:9*
    Your thoughts:

    _____
    _____
    _____

4. *"I have said these things to you, that in me you may have peace. In the world you will have tribulation. But take heart; I have overcome the world." ~ John 16:33 (ESV)*
    What does this verse say about courage?

    _____
    _____
    _____

5. *"Finally, be strong in the Lord and in the strength of his might." ~ Ephesians 6:10 (ESV)*
    How do you get courage according to Ephesians?

    _____
    _____
    _____

<u>Harriet Tubman</u> **(1820-1913).**

https://www.biography.com/people/harriet-tubman-9511430

Tubman escaped from slavery in 1849 and became a famous "conductor" of the Underground Railroad. Tubman risked her life to lead hundreds of slaves to freedom using that secret network of safe houses.

Moral Courage: Persevering under pressure.

"Courage is about doing what you're afraid to do.
There can be no courage unless you're scared.
Have the courage to act instead of react."
~ Oliver Wendell Holmes

Knowing what is right and being courageous to act on situations because of that knowledge is moral courage. Sometimes it might be easier to stand in the face of adversity with one other person who agrees with your stance; be that person someone else can lean on. I remember once speaking up against an issue I felt was wrong. Once I spoke up, several others spoke up to say they felt the same way but were uncomfortable saying anything. Together we changed the entire group policy. Courage won. Be the role model others need to find their own courageous voice.

"Courage doesn't always roar.
Sometimes courage is the little voice at the end of the day
that says I'll try again tomorrow."
~ Mary Anne Rademacher

Standing up for what is right because it is right allows us to like who we see when we look in a mirror and to sleep soundly at night. Maggie Kuhn, a social activist reminds us to, "Speak your mind, even if your voice shakes."

Situational Courage: Layer experiences to define who you are.

Finding opportunities to stand down your fear may unlock forward thinking areas of your mind. If fear blocks you from letting go of the familiar for a run through the unfamiliar then give fear the boot and sprint. Explore. Dream. Test yourself.

Face new adventures, suffering, failure, strange and mysterious with the same passion you would a first love. Defining facets of who you are will be exhilarating and could open new doors you might not have previously considered.

"Man cannot discover new oceans
unless he has the courage to lose sight of the shore."
~Lord Chesterfield

...And neither can courage and self-discovery.

Pick Up Your Sword:

1. Can you think of a time when you were afraid, and you chose to face your fear?

   _____

   How did you feel?

   _____

   What did it teach you?

   _____

2. Have you ever experienced a time when you were afraid, you let your fear get the best of you and either the worst did not happen, or you regretted not facing it?

   _____

   How did it feel?

   _____

   What did it teach you?

   _____

3. Scripture teaches us that fear is the end of faith. What can you do to build your faith up?

   _____

4. Do you think of yourself as courageous or having courage? Why or why not?

   _____

5. What is the next step you can take action on to build inner courage?

   _____

6. What acts of courage inspire you to embrace courage in you?

   _____

7. Do you agree that failure can teach you courage? Why or Why not?

   _____

8. Do you agree that courage is being afraid but moving forward anyway?

   _____

9. What is your worst fear?

   _____

10. Are you ready to face this fear and act to solve it?

_____

Name your fears. Categorize them as rational or irrational. Burn the irrational ones (seek counseling to tame them) and find solutions for the rational ones. Then build your faith by giving them away to Christ. Memorize scripture to quote when fear begins to wage war. Call them out and burst their power with promises that cannot be broken.

_____

_____

_____

_____

_____

Memorize these scripture verses quoting them when fear challenges your faith.

- *"When I am afraid, I will trust in thee." ~ Psalms 56:3*

- *"Peace I leave with you; my peace I give you. I do not give to you as the world gives. Do not let your hearts be troubled and do not be afraid." ~ John 14:27*

- *"Have I not commanded you? Be strong and courageous. Do not be afraid; do not be discouraged, for the LORD your God will be with you wherever you go." ~ Joshua 1:9*

- *"The LORD is my light and my salvation— whom shall I fear? The LORD is the stronghold of my life— of whom shall I be afraid?" ~ Psalm 27:1*

- *"But now, this is what the LORD says— he who created you, Jacob, he who formed you, Israel: "Do not fear, for I have redeemed you; I have summoned you by name; you are mine." ~ Isaiah 43:1*

<u>Mercy Otis Warren</u> (1728-1814).

https://www.britannica.com/biography/Mercy-Otis-Warren

Warren was a writer and propagandist of the American Revolution. She published poems and plays that attacked the British empire and urged colonists to resist Britain's infringement on their rights.

Courageous Confidence

> *"The way to develop self-confidence is to*
> *do the thing you fear and get a*
> *record of successful experiences behind you."*
> *~ William Jennings Bryan*

Many of us desire confidence, but we lack the courage to stretch our comfort zones. Since our level of confidence dictates how we feel about ourselves, we can control our abilities to succeed. Our levels of confidence also set our levels of happiness, but often we stop short of all we can be.

There are many ways to build our self-confidence if we have the courage to explore and embrace living on the edge of other possibilities. We get comfortable with daily routines, things we know and understand, and create "rules" to live by that keep us safe. It takes courage to think outside the box, or to step outside of our comfort zones. By trying one or all of these things, we can build little successes, which in turn build our self-assurance. Going through difficult times creates experiences that build buoyancy for us for the future.

Here are a few things we can be successful at today:

Accept reality: Too often we get caught up in hoping and wishing our lives were different. We desire that people treat us better, but then refuse to hold them accountable when they don't. We allow them to treat us poorly. We wish our finances were better and yet continue to live beyond our means. Or we do not assign every dollar a job and then cannot figure out where the money went. Some of us live in a world where we are waiting for things to improve just because we want them to. Getting real about situations we desire to be different means we need to accept where they are, make a new plan, and then execute it to the best of our ability. Excuse-making and blame-shifting belong as far away from us, and we can make it. It is time to put our big girl panties on and get at making dreams into goals.

Make a plan: Often we are aimless. We say we want to be happy, but we do not know what happy looks like—therefore when it arrives, we may never notice. Put nouns to our wants. By now you have heard of SMART goals. Specific Measurable Attainable Realistic and Timely. Know what you want, write it down, find out if it is attainable or realistic and then set a specific time to meet the goal. Then when your ship comes in, you will actually be on the dock waving it in.

Create a bucket list: Life cannot be all work. We need to dream dreams. Make a list—a bucket list. Then start to move toward completing these items. You will enjoy it three times over. The first time you will enjoy planning it, the second time will be experiencing it, and the third time will be reliving it over and over.

Practice little happies: Do more of what makes you happy, and less of what doesn't. Cut drama out of your life. People who drain you should be moved to the outer edges of your world, and those who energize you should be moved closer to the inner circle of you. Besides the big dreams, make a list of little things you enjoy: fresh coffee in the morning, lavender-scented sheets, soft slippers, lunch with a friend, matching scrunches for your hair, cuddling with a pet, or planting your favorite flower. Find the little happies of life daily and notice them.

Make your bed: Starting your day feeling like you have already accomplished something is a step in the right direction. If the day goes wrong, you still have a neatly made bed to climb into at the end of the day.

Set boundaries: As women, our lives often involve multi-tasking at Mach II with our hair on fire. I laugh when my husband and I say we're going to bed. He gets up and goes to bed. I get up, make sure the doors are locked, the dishwasher is turned on, the dogs have gone outside to do their business, the heater is off, so we do not wake up too hot in the morning, and the cat is inside so we do not have to let her in in the middle of the night. I see you laughing, you know what I'm talking about! So, I have a couple of hard fast rules I live by: NO Crap before 9 a.m. I will not begin phone calls, bill paying, laundry, dishes, or anything else before 9 in the morning. I get up, get my coffee, eat, work out, shower, read, and pray. It is tempting at times to get a head start on the day by starting early, but I've discovered that when I do that, I am unproductive all day long! Respecting myself enough to have a morning start time makes all the difference in the day.

Schedule play: Work hard all week, but schedule play time. I don't mean work-out time, or nap time. I mean play. Call a girlfriend, get out of the house, and do something fun. I have for years practiced BBFF day. That is my Biblical Best Friend Friday. We meet at 1 every Friday. We have no agenda except to find some new adventure. We need women friends to downshift, complain about our life, cheer each other's successes, and to just be girls for a few hours. But if you don't plan for it, life will eat up your play time and you'll drag your tail through just surviving life.

Get your hair done: There is nothing like a new cut and/or color to help us feel on top of the world. It is such a little thing that builds confidence; do it often.

Pick Up Your Sword:

1. *"Strength and dignity are her clothing, and she smiles at the future."*
   ~ Proverbs 31:25
   What does Proverbs 31:25 say true confidence is?

   _____

   _____

   _____

2. *"She makes coverings for herself; her clothing is fine linen and purple."*
   ~ Proverbs 31:22
   What kind of self-care builds confidence? Is it about clothes or something more?

   _____

   _____

   _____

3. *"Beauty to me, is about being comfortable in your own skin...or wearing a kick-ass red lipstick." ~ Gwyneth Paltrow*
   What is Gwyneth talking about and how can you use this information?

   _____

   _____

   _____

born in the Netherlands, raised Jewish, her and her family hid from the Nazis for two years. Anne wrote a diary describing the atrocities of the times held in a museum to educate all of us.

Confidence Under Fire—Adapt the best, drop the rest!

"Low self-confidence isn't a life sentence.
Self-confidence can be learned, practiced,
And mastered—just like any other skill.
Once you master it, everything in your life
Will change for the better."
~Barrie Davenport

Attacking our lives fearlessly requires confidence. We should be comfortable with trying and failing and then readjust based on the new information. When my son was entering high school, he not only played freshman baseball but was also a swing player with the varsity team. The increased speed at the plate was at first hard for him to hit when it was his turn at bat. Time after time, he'd strike out watching the pitches go by. Following a game, I asked him, "Why do you just watch the pitches and not take a chance swinging at it?"

His answer was, "I'm not sure I can hit it."

"Ok, I understand, but each swing of the bat whether you make contact of not is data for your body and brain on how to adjust to the next pitch. If you never swing, you'll never make contact."

So, it goes with many of us. We watch life go by fearful we will not be perfect, or that it just does not feel right. And yet, I have seen women with far less talent become more successful because they are out there doing unafraid of failure.

There are a few traits confident women employ that make them successful.

- **They take care of themselves**. We are no good to anyone unless we're good to ourselves. That might mean a once a week walk-about (get away from your normal routine for a day or several hours). Hit the workout. Meditate. Be alone with your thoughts. Quiet times to pray and clarify direction and responsibilities. Stop seeing these things as luxuries, but rather maintenance.

- **Advocate for yourself**. Listen intently but never blindly. Gather information but then filter it through your own wisdom and needs. Do not raise your family or live your life by others' rules. Modify and adapt the best, drop the rest.

- **Dump the drama, acknowledge the feelings**. As women, we feel things deeply. But because we are women there are times to separate our emotions from the facts. Equally, there are times to put our decisions on hold because our emotions are running the show. Recognizing the real reasons why we are feeling the way we are feeling can typically solve the issue sooner and move us from turmoil to tactical planning.

- **Embrace new experiences**. Look for them, run towards them. Too often we sink into our comfort zones because they are comfortable. We do not grow from this rut and can always return to the norm. But let us not short-change our life experiences. New 'things' help to cut new facets to our souls, making us shine with brilliance.

- **Bring it on attitudes**. We can spend far too much energy and time worrying about the "what-ifs," "should-have" or "could have been" thoughts. You're a strong woman; the event will get taken care of—good or bad. If you do it wrong the first time, do it different the next time. Embrace the "Bring It On" attitude! This way worry must take a backseat to your empowered adventure.

- **No Regrets**. I remember as a young woman deciding that I would so much rather be an old woman reliving my good and bad experiences rather than sitting in my rocking chair wondering what might have happened if I'd tried. Choose life. If you can dream it, give it a try.

- **The tyranny of the urgent shouldn't take priority over the important**. It is midnight on a school night; your teen wants to talk…forget the time, dash the idea of needing sleep for work the next day (unless you're a brain surgeon) and talk. Make a midnight taco run; they will not be your teen forever. So, what if dinner is late. Some rules need to be broken to place the important above the urgent. Choose wisely.

- **Don't ignore your instincts**. Trust that womanly radar that tells you what is right even when others do not think it is. Weigh it, make it answer to your wisdom but give a voice to your gut feelings. They are there for a reason, use them.

- **Silence is golden**. Too many women attempt to fill every open moment with meaningless chatter. In fact, being uncomfortable with silence is the easiest way to assess a woman's confidence. Learn to value alone time as well. Respect yourself enough to spend time by yourself to hear what you think. Evaluate, clarify, and strategize your future. Or use the time to observe others. There is a lot to be learned with your mouth shut!

- **Don't rescue everyone (thing)**. Get comfortable with equipping others to their success. Sometimes that means watching them struggle but remember: If the butterfly did not struggle to squeeze through the small opening in the chrysalis, the life-giving gel will not be distributed through the wings to allow flight. Help for a moment but then hand it back to them. Let their success be their success.

- **Accept criticism with a balancing act**. If the reproach is true, there is no defense for your actions. Fix it. Move on. If the assessment is not true, there is no need to defend yourself. Make a note of the source and decide if perhaps they do not know you well enough or this is about them, not you. The move on.

There is a canyon gap between who you are and what you have. Titles are great for office doors and headstones. But what will live on in the hearts of who you love, and your circle of influence is who you are. At the end of the day, being able to look in the mirror and like who you see is far more valuable than what you own. Understanding the difference can set us free. Take ownership of you.

Pick Up Your Sword:

1. Do you like yourself? Why or why not?
   _____
   _____
   _____

2. Do you take care of yourself? What can you improve on?
   _____
   _____
   _____

3. Come up with 3 responses you can say when tempted to rescue someone rather than equip them for success. For example: A friend poured their heart out to me regarding a tough situation, rather than fix it for her I said, "Wow! That's tough, what are you going to do?" To my child, in the same situation I remember saying, "You're such a good friend, you'll think of something good for them and you." Now write your potential responses to common 'fix it' conversations:
   1 _____
   2 _____
   3 _____

Emily Dickinson

born in 1830 was one of the most famous American female poets. Responsible for founding Amherst College, most of her 1800 poems were not published until after her death.

Lesson 26

Be Fearless!

> *"Everyone thinks of changing the world,*
> *but no one thinks of changing himself."*
> *~Leo Tolsty*

Be Fearless! There will be things you cannot change, but that means there are things you can change. Invest in the things that allow the greatest definition of who you can become and then press on to become all of that. Each of us have been given a gift, and we often mistakenly believe it is for us. Our finest hour is when we have defined our gifts, polished them to a sparkling shine and then handed the blessing over to others.

Artist might at first use broad strokes when creating a masterpiece, but it is the finer details that brings the art to life. Likewise, understanding who we are and where we are going helps define our fearless growth. Looking at fear and trust and how we define them in our day to day lives opens new possibilities. Once you have challenged this step of growth you are in a stronger position to paint your canvas. The artist in you will move toward the truer version of you! Paint that masterpiece!

Emulate

Find someone that is a bit further down life's path than you are. Someone who has overcome their fear of change, defined themselves and their purpose, then ask them how they did it. You'll walk away with golden tidbits to use on your journey. People want to see us succeed. Your Designer wants you to be all you can be.

Who's the thief in your life?

We often look for reasons outside of ourselves for our lack of feeling fulfilled and purpose filled. Truth is, we are usually our own stumbling blocks. We hold ourselves back or are afraid to define our talents. We might need to re-define ourselves, remove excuses and stop settling for our mediocrity.

Learned patterns from childhood may hold us captive to old ideas of who we are or who we are supposed to be. Survival may have been your only defining thought. It's time to realize you are better than those old beliefs and it's time to take your rightful place in blessing the world by becoming who you have been fearfully designed to be.

Perhaps you were raised with the good-girl syndrome and are afraid to take risks, keeping you captive to people-pleasing. Try to see your life through adult eyes rather than the rules you have now outgrown. These rules were once good guidelines but may no longer fit situations now.

Trauma can also stunt our maturity. Until we deal with it, we will remain the emotional age we were when the trauma took place. Take the time to define the situations, discover the right and wrong of it; then plan to move forward with the lesson it teaches. This may be as simple as acknowledging what happened or perhaps years in the making learning new skills to move out of the past and into the present. Whatever it takes, strategize to move forward in your own definition of who you are and what matters to you.

We might even try living our lives by someone else's interpretations. We move with their rules, we believe what they believe. There is nothing wrong with starting out that way, but there must be a time when we question everything and make it answer to who we are becoming.

Perhaps you have been through the trauma of divorce, been abused or struggle with addictions. Not only do these ordeals create suffering, dependence, slanted and shallow thinking, but they stunt emotional maturity. They can kill our confidence and shatter our self-esteem.

Ask yourself: Who is the thief in your life? We often look for reasons outside of ourselves for our lack of feeling fulfilled and purposeful. Truth is, we are usually our own stumbling blocks. We hold ourselves back or are afraid to define our talents. We might need to re-define ourselves, remove excuses and stop settling for our mediocrity.

Pick up your sword:

1. *"What shall we then say to these things? If God be for us, who can be against us?" ~ Romans 8:31 (KJV)*
    What does this verse say to you?

    _____

    _____

    _____

2. Emulate: Find someone that has overcome their fear of change, defined themselves and their purpose, then ask them how they did it. You will walk away with golden tidbits to use on your journey. People want to see you succeed. Your Designer wants you to be all you can be.

    Who will your person be? _____

3. List your fears: Make a list of all the things that keep you from being successful.

_____

_____

_____

4. Now list things you can do to bring about change. You might discover that the simple act of writing them down, helps you acknowledge them, and solve them.

_____

_____

_____

5. What is your superpower? (If you don't know, ask others…they'll see it often before we do!)

_____

_____

_____

Indira Gandhi, (1917-1984),

https://www.history.com/topics/india/indira-gandhi

born in 1917 in India was the 3rd Prime Minister of India and worked hard as an influential politician. She was assassinated in October of 1984 by her own bodyguards following her orders to military action in the Golden Temple in Operation Blue Star.

To Trust or Not to Trust?

"Trust take years to build,
Seconds to break and forever to repair."
~ Dhar Mann

We've all been taught to trust adults when we're young. We are told to trust authority when we're entering the world, we trust our hearts with relationships, and perhaps past performance when it comes to business relationships, but what does trust look like?

Trust comes in a variety of packages. It takes a trained eye to recognize authenticity. We tend to want to trust people implicitly, but tough experiences tend to teach that we need to give people room to prove themselves.

More importantly, learning to trust ourselves is the rudder that directs the ship out to sea. Trusting our inner voice at first is difficult. When I began to dissect myself, I had to untangle who I believed I was verses who I had been told I was. There were too many voices in my head describing me. I had to learn to trust myself first to trust others. It is a process we all need to walk through.

When we are young we first need to try on different personalities, philosophies of life, and emulate those we admire most. Eventually though, we need to form our own opinions as to who we are rather than who others think we are, or who we are told to be. We can become stuck in our personalities because we have not explored what thoughts belong to us and which ones have been handed to us. We don't trust ourselves to be ourselves, but we need to.

What makes us trustworthy?

Here are a few ways to build trust worthiness:

- **Do what you say you'll do**. A person who over-promises and only rarely delivers, is not someone others can put their trust in. People need to know that we think through what we are going to do before we commit. It gives others confidence in us and our word. As much as we would love to be all things to all people, it's never going to be doable. Use an old sales adage I was taught—under promise and over-deliver.

- **Over Communicate**. Often what we say is not what the other person heard. Without being condescending, ask them to tell you what you just said to be certain you are communicating clearly. Honest communication builds trust that others can bank on. It gives others a chance to know us so well that when they hear something 'off' they will recognize there is a problem because we would never do 'that.'

- **Value the people around you**. We might think everyone around us, including family, friends, and co-workers, know exactly how much we value them. Truth is, most do not, unless we tell them often and in various ways. You need to be careful we do not take them for granted—it's easy to do. When we are under stress or uber busy, look up, live in the moment, and remind our support that we cannot get life done well without them.

- **Prioritize Honesty**. Tell the truth even when it hurts. Being less than honest builds shaky relationships. Lying says either, "I don't think you are strong enough to handle the truth" or "I don't value you enough to be honest with you." We think we are helping by hiding or dressing up the truth when in fact we are dishonoring the person and destroying our integrity.

- **Serve others but set boundaries**. Stepping back from our own priorities speaks volumes to an individual that we care about them enough to put them at the top of the list of things 'to do.' Serving cheerfully restates that they are valuable. Overdoing for a person says we do not think you're capable and sets a situation that can cause them to be dependent. Find a balance. Serve, but do not cripple them.

- **Be true to you**. People want to know we care. When we share our emotions —good, bad, or ugly—we build a bridge that allows them in. If we hide our emotions under the guise of being professional or strong, we dig a moat between us and them. If we are hurt, it's okay to be sad. If we're upset don't pretend we're not. Body language is easy to read; so, when our body tells a different message than our words, we are not trustworthy. On the flip side, people who live in their emotions constantly are equally difficult to trust. Be true to our feelings but if a situation calls for a reaction on a scale of 1-10 and we are always reacting as a 9 or 10, not only are we hard to trust but we're exhausting, and relationships will break down.

- **Don't Fling Your Resume**. Johnny Appleseed's dad use to tell him, "If there's any bragging to be done about you, let someone else be doing it!" There are times to self-promote, but if we always command the floor, it's time to step back and notice the other people in the room. Look, we all want to be the hero in our own stories but lifting others up will bring life to a room and the 'braggin' will be done by them.

- **Believe enough in your values to be true to them**. When we build a reputation of doing what we believe to be right, even when others disagree with us, they may not like our stance, but they will respect our choices and our consistent veracity. It makes us reliable when we stick to what we believe is true. If we have chameleon principles, we become fickle and unpredictable. We become a risk. There is a saying that goes, "If you stand for nothing, you'll fall for anything." We must stick to our foundational beliefs. After all, if people see us sell out, they expect then that we would sell out on them.

- **Be quick to say we are wrong**. All of us make mistakes. Be the first one to admit that you failed or were hurtful. This goes back to the same reasons to be honest. Not admitting guilt particularly if it's obvious, makes us look immature and that means we are no longer trustworthy.

If we can practice these few simple strategies, we will experience a life of calm security. We will not have to remember a lie we might have told; we won't have to ask for forgiveness for being mean, we won't have to feel like a wave on shifting sand, and we won't have to worry about being abandoned when those around us feel under-valued.

Building trust starts with being trustworthy. People young and old get behind a person with honorable convictions and who takes the time to build relationships that can be depended on. Challenge yourself to be the most trustworthy person you know!

Pick Up Your Sword:

1. *"When I am afraid, I put my trust in you. In God, whose word I praise, in God I trust; I shall not be afraid. What can flesh do to me?" ~ Psalm 56:3-4*
   What does this verse say about placing our trust?

   _____

   _____

   _____

2. *"Therefore, I tell you, whatever you ask in prayers, believe that you have received it, and it will be yours." ~ Mark 11:24*
   Why are we able to ask and trust?

   _____

   _____

   _____

3. *"They will have no fear of bad news; their hearts are steadfast, trusting in the Lord." ~ Psalm 112:7*
   How can you stay secure in trust according to this verse?

   _____

   _____

   _____

4. *"A gossip betrays a confidence, but a trustworthy person keeps a secret."*
    ~ Proverbs 11:13
    What tip does this verse give you to being a trustworthy person?

    _____

    _____

    _____

5. *"Those who trust in their riches will fail, but the righteous will thrive like a*
    green leaf." ~ Isaiah 43:1
    What tip does this verse give about being a trustworthy person?

    _____

    _____

    _____

6. To be trusted, you must be transparent and authentic. Are you?

    _____

    _____

    _____

7. To be trustworthy, you must set and respect boundaries. Do you?

    _____

    _____

    _____

To build trust, you must: keep your word and commitments, be on time, be
honest (even when it does not benefit you), when you make a mistake admit
it. List 5 more things that will make you trustworthy.

    a. _____

    b. _____

    c. _____

    d. _____

    e. _____

Mother Teresa, (1910- 1997),

https://motherteresa.org/biography.html

the Roman Catholic nun, one of the most admirable women in the world, served the poor and ill individuals. She founded the Missionaries of Charity in Calcutta. She won a Nobel Peace Prize for her service.

For Such a Time as This—Facing the Challenges Life Brings

"People are like stained-glass windows.
They sparkle and shine when the sun is out,
but when the darkness sets in,
their true beauty is revealed only if there is light from within."
~Elisabeth Kübler-Ross

2020 was a tough year. We were challenged in a wide variety of ways. Each of us has a story to tell about a year of ups and downs; some good, some not so good events and situations. We stand at a crossroad demanding we choose a path that may not have been our first choice. Yet here we stand.

Esther was a woman in a similar challenge. Read Esther 1-9.

Her story:

Esther, the Bible's Cinderella story, was beautiful, an orphan and loved by everyone who met her. Raised by her cousin, Mordecai, and groomed to be a queen by a eunuch named Hegai, she was chosen to step into royalty following the removal of Queen Vashti.

King Ahasuerus was not a Prince Charming. He was a drunk who loved to show off his wealth and power. He hosted a feast for everyone in the 127 provinces he ruled over. He encouraged them all to drink to excess. At the peak of partying one night, he summoned his queen, Vashti. She was beautiful and had a great figure. He ordered her to show up to the party to show her off. Shocked by being treated like a trophy, she refused. (we will talk about her in another study)

The King's advisors approached him, appalled that a wife would disobey a husband's orders. They feared this news would go viral and would usher in widespread disobedience in the land by other wives. Vashti was banned from the kingdom and the search for another queen began.

All the young virgins were rounded up and brought to a house called the Woman's House. Hegai, the eunuch, oversaw the women and trained them in the ways of beauty treatments. He taught them how to eat, skin treatments and how to use oils to enhance their beauty. He spent six months preparing the 'contestants' before they could meet the King. Esther was well liked by Hegai and he granted her special favors and educated her in the ways of the palace.

When the time came, Hegai sent each woman to the King to spend the night with him. They returned the next morning to the Woman's House. Each one vied for the 'first wife' position…sort of an Old Testament 'The Bachelor' series! Once the women returned, they remained the rest of their lives in the second wives' home, unable to return to their families. Following Vashti's departure women were forbidden to approach the King. If they did, they could be put to death. They lived their lives in the palace awaiting a summons by the King.

The King loved Esther and made her queen. He threw a huge celebration in her honor. Racial divisions during this period were significant and her cousin had instructed her to keep her ethnicity a secret to avoid prejudice or danger. Although of Jewish decent, Esther's appearance did not give her ancestry away.

Mordecai worked at the King's gate and overheard a plot involving two of the King's eunuchs who planned to kill the King. Mordecai told Queen Esther who secretly shared it with the King. Following an investigation, the story was found to be true. Both men were impaled on pointed poles. Mordecai's information helped build favor in the King's eyes for Esther.

Haman, the King's right-hand man, was promoted to the head of all the officials. On the King's orders, everyone would kneel and bow face down to Haman. Mordecai did not bow down, and the other workers noticed. When they asked him why, he explained he was a Jew and could not bow to another God. The gossip spread to Haman.

Haman went to King Ahasuerus claiming that the Jews in his kingdom governed themselves by their own laws and would not obey the King's laws. The King, taken to listening to many around him, agreed to let Haman deal with the problem and gave him his royal ring to seal the deal. Haman set a law in place that all Jews should be put to death. The decree was sent out to all 127 provinces ordering on the 13th day of the 12th month every Jew—man, woman, and child—should be sought out and put to death. The kingdom of Susa was in shock.

When Mordecai read the order, he tore his clothes, put ashes on his head and wore mourning clothes. The Jewish community sobbed in anguish. Esther's handmaids hurried to tell Esther about Mordecai. She sent a trusted eunuch to find out what was going on. Mordecai told the servant everything and sent a copy of the order to kill every Jew back with the messenger for Esther to see. Mordecai's message to Esther was to go to the King to stop this order.

Esther sent word back to Mordecai that the law said anyone who entered the King's inner court without being summoned would be put to death, and that the King had not called her in the previous 30 days.

Mordecai responded, "What makes you think you will escape this death sentence?" He warned that, "their help would come from somewhere else, and her new family would be put to death by the rescuers if she identified with royalty."

Then he said something that caused her to pick up her sword: ***"Perhaps it is for such a time as this that you have been chosen."***

Esther asked Mordecai to gather all the Jews and to fast and pray for three days for her courage. Three days later, she put on her royal clothes and stood in the entry of the inner court. When the King noticed her, he smiled and summoned her asking, "What is it Queen Esther? I'll give you anything up to half my kingdom."

She requested he come and bring Haman to a feast she had prepared for him, and then she would answer his question. Haman was thrilled at receiving the invitation and on his way home ran into Mordecai who would not kneel or bow to him. Haman seethed. On the advice of friends and Haman's wife, he had a 75-foot pointed pole constructed in plans to impale Mordecai on it.

The night before Esther's feast, the King could not sleep. He called his servants to him to read reports. When they came to the section where Mordecai had revealed the plan to have the king killed, the king asked, "What honor was done for him?"

The servants replied, "Nothing."

About this same time, Haman arrived to tell the King to impale Mordecai on the pole he had constructed but the King asked him first, "What shall be done for a man I really want to honor?"

Haman responded, "Have servants bring out a robe that the King himself has worn, place it on him and put him on a horse with the king's crest and have a servant lead them through the town honoring him."

The King declared, "Do this now for Mordecai."

Haman did as he was told and returned home ashamed and embarrassed.

The King and Haman attended a second feast with Esther and this time the King begged her to tell him what she wanted. She finally said, "If it pleases the King, give me my life and the lives of my people."

Shocked the King said, "Who is this person that would take your life?"

Esther replied, "A man who hates and is your enemy—Haman!"

The King was furious. A servant spoke up, "There is a pole in Haman's yard built to impale Mordecai on." The King commanded that Haman be impaled on it immediately.

Esther then bowed in tears at the King's feet and pleaded with him to write a new law rescinding the one created to kill all the Jews. In his agony, he explained, royal tradition held that a law could not be undone. Searching to right this wrong, instead, he gave Mordecai his royal ring and said, "You decide what makes this right. Whatever you decree and seal with the ring, will be."

Mordecai wrote a law allowing the Jews the right to defend themselves from Haman's law. Word got around the provinces of Mordecai's great power and how the

King had honored him and the demise of Haman. They were afraid of Mordecai's great influence and many of them sided (converted) with the Jews. All those who hated Jews were killed, including Haman's ten sons.

What can we learn from Esther?

Imagine being a young woman of marriageable age (12-13 yrs. old) hoping to be the chosen one to bare the Christ child (like all her peers) but instead being taken from your home by your sworn enemy to be groomed to be a wife for a King you don't know. It took great courage on Esther's part to adapt to her situation. She must have matured from a girl to a woman over night to win the King's favor. Esther faced her potential death to save her people knowing the previous Queen Vashti had been cast aside for lesser stands.

- The right way to fight.
- God uses ordinary people to accomplish great things.
- Esther did not allow her difficult situation to make her bitter
- Esther knew how to rally the troops to help her (fast & Pray)
- She did not let her beauty make her prideful
- Great example of bravery (even if your first response isn't)
- How to use wise counsel (she knew where to find her strength)
- To surround yourself with wise counsel.
- To be kind enough that those in authority help you toward your goal.
- That God is working behind the scenes even when we don't see it or understand it. Trusting Him allows His divine purpose to occur.

Pick Up Your Sword:

1. *"And let us consider how we may spur one another on toward love and good deeds," ~ Hebrews 10:25 (NIV)*
   What does Hebrews 10:24 instruct us to do with all types of people?

   _____

   _____

   _____

2. *"A new command I give you: Love one another. As I have loved you, so you must love one another."* ~ *John 13:34 (NIV)*
   What does John 13:34 tell us about caring for each other? Are there restrictions on who we should love?

   _____

   _____

   _____

3. *"So, God created mankind in his own image, in the image of God he created them; male and female he created them."* ~ *Genesis 1:27 (NIV)*

   "...and through your offspring all nations on earth will be blessed because you have obeyed me." ~ *Genesis 22:18 (NIV)*
   What does God say about race? Genesis 1:27, Genesis 22:18

   _____

   _____

   _____

4. Considering our own circle of influence, if we are part of a minority group, what experience, lessons, and wisdom can you share with those around us to give more birth to equality?

   _____

   _____

   _____

5. If you are part of a so called 'dominant culture' what can be done to allow more space for other cultures to be heard?

   _____

   _____

   _____

6. Think about it: Perhaps it is race, maybe it is politics or perhaps the divided opinions of Covid-19 and how we handle them: What one thing can you do differently today to bring equality and peace to a world desperately in need?

   _____

   _____

   _____

Perhaps you have been created for such a time as this!
What's stopping you?

Summary by Fay C. Acker:

"Esther, a Jew, could not be seen for who she was in the fullness of being "marvelously set apart" by God. (Psalms 139:14) She and her people were profiled because of race and religion; she had to deny who she was for her own safety. Esther was called to identify with the suffering of her race, resist injustice, and cross racial boundaries to save her people and help others to live in line with God's vision.

All lives matter to God, all of us are "Marvelously set apart" for God's glory, but some lives in our society have been valued more than others. We have witnessed horrendous acts of cruelty throughout history because of humanity's refusal to see "the other' through God's eyes. When we refuse to recognize the goodness of God's creation in someone of another race, we are debasing God's own creation and limiting possibilities for the world.

Like Esther, we have come "for a moment like this" and have the opportunity to be reconcilers and healers for God. As women of God, we do not close our eyes to injustice and suffering, but we look with courage at ourselves and society through the eyes of God who loves us all."

<u>Princess Diana</u>, **(1961-1997),**

https://www.biography.com/royalty/princess-diana

married to Prince Charles grew to be the 'People's Princess'. Mother to William and Harry, she impacted the world by caring for people most passed over. She died in a tragic car crash while chased by paparazzi.

Faith or Fear?

> *"The thief comes only to steal and kill and destroy;*
> *I came so that they would have life and have it abundantly."*
> *~John 10:10 (NASB)*

Where do we start? This is about going on a journey, an adventure where your faith is bigger than your fear. It's about moving away from the unknown and moving toward the known—your purpose in life.

The average age women live today is 84 years of age. Now subtract your age from that. If you are 30 right now, you have 54 years to make your mark in the world. Sounds like a long time huh. But think back on your high school graduation, and it feels like yesterday, right? That is how quickly time goes by. We need to embrace who we are created to be. All of it. Too often we sell ourselves short, we do not believe we measure up or that we are worthy of more. It is time to realize, if we're still here, we're not done. The days we have left need to be spent in the fullness of who we are for the benefit of our purpose. If we do not do what we are gifted to do who will we leave in our absence?

We spend so much time worried about what others think of us, and letting our thoughts run like mice on an exercise wheel. We exhaust ourselves and go no-where. Practice being present in the moment. That means being okay with sitting still, taking a breath, observing people and your surroundings.

I once was challenged to take ten minutes each day to just be still. I thought, "No big deal," until I tried it. I set a timer on my phone and sat beside our koi pond. I was surprised at how long ten minutes feels like. I worked to clear my mind and just observe my surroundings. I lasted three minutes. I tried the second day with only slightly more success. It took me nearly a week to sit quietly and peacefully for ten minutes doing nothing but meditating.

The more we can be aware around us, the richer our lives will be. We will notice things that we don't typically notice. We can learn to listen more to our loved ones, notice strangers and meet their needs with random acts of kindness.

We need to start loving ourselves the way our maker loves us. We need to feel worthy of love enough to forgive our pasts and be bold enough to live our futures. We are what we think we are, so speaking the truths about ourselves will let our worth sink from our heads to our hearts.

Pick Up Your Sword:

1. Write down affirmations, put them on post it notes and place them all over your home. Then read them aloud daily. Write down 5 here:

   _____

   _____

   _____

   _____

   _____

2. Do more things you love and eliminate the things you do not. If it brings joy, keep it. If it brings stress to your life, find a way to lose it.
   What do you need to lose today?

   _____

   _____

   _____

3. Evaluate how you spend your 24 hours a day. Get rid of wasted time and fill those spaces with quality events. Perhaps your time will be spent playing with your kids, walking a field with your faithful pet, fishing, trying a new recipe with a family member that loves to cook, that exercise class you keep talking about, read a book, coach a sport, sew a quilt, plant a flower. What will yours be?

   _____

   _____

   _____

4. Learn to put yourself first so you can be filled up for others. If that means eating right, getting sleep, delegating more, and taking time away, then do it. A huge ship can set sail across the ocean, but it needs a rudder to direct it. You are that rudder. What will your first self-care be?

   _____

   _____

   _____

5. Watch how you treat others, inspire them to help you. Teach them how to treat you and engage in your purpose. The example you set may just demonstrate how to attain their fulfillment. Name yours:

   _____

   _____

   _____

6. There's power in words—good and bad. If you are a person who speaks negatively about life, others and yourself—STOP! If you are not accustomed to thinking positively of yourself, start doing it and do it more than you think is normal. What negative thoughts or speech will you replace today?

_____

_____

_____

7. If you have a victim mentality—STOP! If you are not sure, ask others that you trust will tell you the truth. There is a time to be a victim, but staying there exhaust you, others and pulls you away from your best self. If you were a victim, do what you must do to leave it behind: counseling, removing yourself from situations, refreshing your thinking or confronting the problem. What did you learn and what will you do about it?

_____

_____

_____

Start today, to get to know you, identify your strengths, admit your weaknesses, and build them up, be more still than busy, and let the creator who knit you in the womb show you the fullness of who you are and the circle of influence that belongs to only you.

1. What are your strengths?

_____

_____

_____

2. What are your weaknesses?

_____

_____

_____

3. Can you turn a weakness into a strength? How will you?

_____

_____

_____

Malala Yousafzai,

https://www.biography.com/activist/malala-yousafzai

on October 9th, 2012 a gunman shot her three times in the head for speaking out about education for girls. She changed the course of women's rights and was awarded the Nobel Peace Prize. She said, "I don't want to be remembered as the girl who was shot. I want to be remembered as the girl who stood up."

Choosing to be Authentic

"When you are authentic, you create a certain energy…
people want to be around you because you are unique."
– Andie MacDowell

As women, we naturally are caretakers of the people and lives around us. Though I applaud our nurturing roles, we can accomplish loving others and loving ourselves without compromising ourselves. Without a strong sense of who we are created to be, we can get lost in the demands of others and do what is convenient or fulfilling for them. After a time, we lose even the desire to fight for our authentic self because we have built a world and expectations from others around this pretender allowed to live in place of our true self.

When asked, "Who are you?" most people tell us what they do…I am a teacher, a mom, a plumber, a cashier, a lawyer, etc. They tell us what they do, not who they are. They cannot tell you who they are because they have not defined themselves. They have not asked themselves the hard questions or they do not know the questions to ask. Often, they simply do not know who they are yet.

Discovering your Badass self or our genuine self requires looking from the inside out. We may be imitating who we think we should be or who we think the world says we should be. There is a time and a place for imitating who we want to be, but there is also a time when that practice stops serving us. We waste the time and unique talents we bring to the world. When we know there is more to us and chose to stay where we are, we become imposters. Imposters waste giftings, talents, deny inner joy and the energy to pursue life as we were designed to do. Worse, we give up control of our inner self and are tossed on a whim to be what the outside definitions demand.

Being an On Purpose Person!

Each new year gives us an opportunity to start new, to become a person that lives life intentionally. Living on purpose might mean many things to many people for me it means simplifying where I spend my time, money, energy, and passions. I want to be healthy physically, spiritually, emotionally, socially, and spend my energy on things that will make a lasting difference in this world. I took some time to decide goals for the year for all things important.

The STRATEGY techniques listed below will not give you the answers to your goals, but they may help you build the foundation to start.

Still – Sit intentionally quiet. Ask yourself, if failure were no option and I have already succeeded, what would I be passionate about doing? How am I unique to my product or business? How will I pass that on?

Tools – Do what you must do to acquire the tools you need to do what you want to do. Set up your office to promote efficiency. If that means buying a new pc, then do it. If it means purchasing software, then do it. Having the proper tools will save you time and allow you to do what only you can do.

Research — There is a saying out there that says, "Inspect what you expect." Often people dream about building a business, setting personal goals, or achievements, but they fail to research thoroughly. I had a student once that planned to spend 100K for a college education that would net a job that paid $45K annually. Once they discovered the day-to-day workings of the job, and the amount of top pay they could receive, they wisely chose another profession and another college.

Ask for help — Follow and engage with others that are doing what you want to do. Mentorships can cut your learning curve to success in half by sharing with you the strengths and pitfalls of your desire. Share with them your plan (the one you created in the first step here) and get their opinion on your strategy.

Training — Do not take a shotgun approach to your training. Because you have taken time to research what you want to do, and have asked others, you will have a strong idea of the training needed. Then get the training. Once you have become an expert in your field, then remember your roots and pass on the training to someone else lower on the ladder than yourself.

Energize your passion — Inspiration will look different for each person; seek what works for you to be excited about the hard climb you are embarking on.

Give back — Once you have become an expert in your field, and earning income you can share, be certain to return what you have been given. You might share your finances, your knowledge, your time volunteering where help is needed.

You first, then others — There is a reason that airlines tell you in an emergency to place your mask on your face, then on your child's—without you, the child suffers. I have learned to take time and care of myself in order to keep it all going for the rest of my family. I had to fight with feeling guilty, but now I understand that a ship cannot sail out to sea if it is taking on water or sinking.

Pick Up Your Sword:

1. What part of the strategy do you need to improve on?

    _____

    _____

    _____

2. What does living intentionally mean to you?

    _____

    _____

    _____

3. Do something that brings you joy. Intentional living means being deliberate with your day. Be clear about the results you want for the day. What are they?

    _____

    _____

    _____

4. To be intentional you need to encourage personal growth. What does that look like for you?

    _____

    _____

    _____

5. Take time to define your personal beliefs and then evaluate how you line up with those beliefs. Do you need to add or take away people or activities?

    _____

    _____

    _____

born to an affluent British family, her mother belonged to elite social circles, but Florence not interested in social climbing, she committed to nursing soldiers. She set the standards for nursing during a time when women were to be seen and not heard.

Lesson 31

You have one job!

"There is no greater gift you can give or receive
than to honor your calling.
It's why you were born.
And how you become most truly alive.
~Oprah Winfrey

Once we know who we are and what our purpose is, decision making becomes easier. Our job is to fulfill our purpose by serving others with our gifting, energy, learning style, love language and passion. We're told in Deuteronomy 6:5 to Love the Lord our God with all our heart and with all our soul and with all our might. That means knowing what our purpose in the world is and understanding what our number one job is: To bring as many people to heaven as we are able. All the other things we do must funnel toward this one goal.

I once was involved in a discussion that turned to a confrontation. We were in Palm Springs during the Dinah Shore days. I was eager to go to the marketplace but was told the place would be packed with gays. My response was, "I don't mind crowds." The other person launched into a twenty-minute rant about not wanting to be around 'those' people. I asked for clarification of 'those' people. What I heard next was rhetoric of the thoughtless kind and a question, "How can you not be bothered by this?"

My response was, "I am a Christian first, I am not judge and jury."

His response was, "I guess I'm just old fashioned."

I answered, "If you are so convinced that gay people are not saved, why wouldn't you be there attempting to demonstrate the value of being saved? Your actions and attitudes will not inspire anyone to want the God you serve. The same would be true for thieves, thugs, greedy people and liars."

This is true of everyone, our lifestyle attitudes and actions will either win others or be the very reason they have no interest in understanding the gift God has freely given. And when reading the instruction book Christ left for us there are countless stories where He went out of His way to engage people society thought less than important: tax collectors, prostitutes, thieves, murderers, and demon possessed. It is time for all of us to practice drawing a circle that is inclusive.

As Christians we have one main job—get as many to heaven as possible!

Pick Up Your Sword:

1. *"Let us hold fast the confession of our hope without wavering, for he who promised is faithful. And let us consider how to stir up one another to love and good works, not neglecting to meet together, as is the habit of some, but encouraging one another, and all the more as you see the Day drawing near." ~ Hebrews 10:23-25*

   What does Hebrews say is our job or purpose here on earth?

   _____

   _____

   _____

2. *"If then there is any encouragement in Christ, any consolation from love, any sharing in the Spirit, any compassion and sympathy, make my joy complete: be of the same mind, having the same love, being in full accord and of one mind. Do nothing from selfish ambition or conceit, but in humility regard others as better than yourselves. Let each of you look not to your own interests, but to the interests of others. Let the same mind be in you that was in Christ Jesus, who, though he was in the form of God, did not regard equality with God as something to be exploited, but emptied himself, taking the form of a slave, being born in human likeness. And being found in human form, he humbled himself and became obedient to the point of death—even death on a cross." ~ Philippians 2:1-8*

   What does Philippians say is our job?

   _____

   _____

   _____

3. *"For by grace you have been saved through faith, and this is not your own doing; it is the gift of God—not the result of works, so that no one may boast. For we are what he has made us, created in Christ Jesus for good works, which God prepared beforehand to be our way of life." ~ Ephesians 2:8-10*

   What does Ephesians say about our purpose?

   _____

   _____

   _____

4. *"As God's chosen ones, holy and beloved, clothe yourselves with compassion, kindness, humility, meekness, and patience. Bear with one another and, if anyone has a complaint against another, forgive each other; just as the Lord has forgiven you, so you also must forgive. Above all, clothe yourselves with love, which binds everything together in perfect harmony. And let the peace of Christ rule in your hearts, to which indeed you were called in the one body. And be thankful. Let the word of Christ dwell in you richly; teach and admonish one another in all wisdom; and with gratitude in your hearts sing psalms, hymns, and spiritual songs to God. And whatever you do, in word or deed, do everything in the name of the Lord Jesus, giving thanks to God the Father through him." ~ Colossians 3: 15-17 (ESV)*

How are we to live our lives according to Colossians?

_____

_____

_____

5. *"Brothers, I do not consider that I have made it my own. But one thing I do: forgetting what lies behind and straining forward to what lies ahead, I press on toward the goal for the prize of the upward call of God in Christ Jesus." ~ Philippians 3:13-14*

What does Paul teach us in this verse?

_____

_____

_____

6. *"A brother offended is harder to be won over than a strong city." ~ Proverbs 18:19*

What does this verse warn us about?

_____

_____

_____

Erma Bombeck, 1927-1996,

https://www.goodreads.com/author/show/11882.Erma_Bombeck

"If you can't make it better, you can laugh at it."

Always ready with a quick wit and true to life humor she was an outstanding columnist. She was a wonderful wife and mother and although she struggled through a great deal of pain her last few years, she managed to bring joy and laughter to the world regardless."

Defining Wisdom

"Wisdom comes from making mistakes,
Having the courage to face them,
And make adjustments moving forward
based upon the knowledge acquired through those experiences."
~ Ken Poirot

Recognizing when others do not have or embrace wisdom will save frustration as well as color our method of imparting wisdom. When a person lacks wisdom, it can often be like explaining a retirement plan to a kindergartener; it's useless and inappropriate.

Accessing why a person lacks wisdom can be valuable for understanding their life-experience, their maturity, or perhaps a narcissistic trait.

Here's a few ways to recognize those who lack wisdom:

- They create controversies.
- They're quickly broken beyond healing.
- Lying comes easily to them.
- They're often involved in some kind of trouble.
- They think they're smarter/better than others.
- The are the source of conflict within a family.
- They don't seek others' advice.
- They don't know what they stand for, so they are often easily influenced by multiple opinions or they simply repeat things they've heard without researching the truth.
- They often have lost their positive spirit and childlike wonder.

A person lacking wisdom is:

"Who, with perversion in his heart, continually devises evil,
Who spreads strife.
¹⁵ Therefore his disaster will come suddenly;
Instantly he will be broken and there will be no healing.
¹⁶ There are six things that the Lord hates,
Seven that are an abomination to Him:
¹⁷ Haughty eyes, a lying tongue,
And hands that shed innocent blood,
¹⁸ A heart that devises wicked plans,
Feet that run rapidly to evil,
¹⁹ A false witness who declares lies,
And one who spreads strife among brothers."
~Proverbs 6:14-19

Pick Up Your Sword:

1. *"Who plots evil with deceit in his heart—he always stirs up conflict. Therefore, disaster will overtake him in an instant; he will suddenly be destroyed—without remedy. There are six things the Lord hates, seven that are detestable to him: haughty eyes, a lying tongue, hands that shed innocent blood, a heart that devises wicked schemes, feet that are quick to rush into evil, a false witness who pours out lies and a person who stirs up conflict in the community." ~ Proverbs 6:14-19*
   What can we learn from Proverbs 6:14-19?

   _____

   _____

   _____

2. *"If any of you lacks wisdom, let him ask God, who gives generously to all without reproach, and it will be given him." ~ James 1:5*
   What does James 1:5 promise us?

   _____

   _____

   _____

3. *"Blessed is the one who finds wisdom, and the one who gets understanding, for the gain from her is better than gain from silver and her profit better than gold. She is more precious than jewels, and nothing you desire can compare with her. Long life is in her right hand; in her left hand are riches and honor. Her ways are ways of pleasantness, and all her paths are peace..."*
~ *Proverbs 3:13-18*
Your thoughts on wisdom:

_____

_____

_____

4. *"Listen to advice and accept instruction, that you may gain wisdom in the future." ~ Proverbs 19:20*
What does Proverbs say we should do?

_____

_____

_____

5. *"The way of a fool is right in his own eyes, but a wise man listens to advice."*
~ *Proverbs12:14 (ESV)*
Your thoughts:

_____

_____

_____

6. What do we know from Scripture about how to acquire wisdom?

_____

_____

_____

<u>Maria Montessori</u>, **(1870-1952)**,

https://www.britannica.com/biography/Maria-Montessori

One of the first women to earn a medical degree from the University of Rome. She used her education to create learning techniques for mentally retarded children up through normal range children. Her experience-centered learning style is still used in early childhood learning centers today, called the Montessori Method.

The Value of Painful Growth

"Growth demands a temporary surrender of security.
It may mean giving up familiar but limiting patterns,
safe but unrewarding work, values no longer believed in,
and relationships that have lost their meaning."
~John Maxwell

Growth defined by the dictionary is a process of developing either physically, mentally, or spiritually, or all of these elements. Growth helps us define our maturity by growing the necessary and eliminating the unnecessary. Growth often is disguised by pain, frustration, and loss. Sometimes we need to go through loss to value what we have. And pain often pushes us out of our comfort zones. Though uncomfortable, we find opportunities to emerge better and wiser than before.

Nothing happens when we remain in our comfort zone. A body builder cannot lift the same amount of weight and expect to grow muscle. They must lift beyond their comfort level to tear down or injure a muscle, to repair it and become stronger. And so, it goes with our hearts and souls.

We may experience growth at the hands of someone we thought was an advocate or friend. Honestly, pain can just suck. Try not to react immediately. Take a moment to be aware of the situation and process the other person's perspective. We all have a story, and it may be their past that is causing them to hurt you. If they have hurt you unintentionally, then forgive them quickly and move on. If the hurt was intentional, it might be best to let the relationship move to a further distance in your life. Either way, forgive them. Forgiveness releases the other person's control over your life and allows you to handle the situation with more grace. I have often prayed, "Lord, help me to see them the way you see them." And when I pray for someone, it is tough to continue being upset at them.

I hate that the very lessons that make us wise are so uncomfortable and close to the heart. I remember when my best friend died...,I was 26, she was 30,it hurt so badly that I swore I'd never have another BFF, and in my immature thinking I thought I would avoid any future pain. I helped raise her two children and when her daughter was killed by a drunk driver coming home from work, I double swore I was never going to get close to anyone again to protect my heart. Little did I know that those painful events dug a trench in my heart that allowed me to love deeper than I ever had before. It also taught me to live each day as if I did not have tomorrow. Oftentimes, the very thing that causes us pain builds wisdom in us in unexpected ways. God often uses this added growth and maturity in our lives to minister to others who are hurting.

When God calls warriors to the front lines, there is extensive training that comes with it and most of that training either grows us up or pushes us out of our comfort zones. God has a plan, but He cannot heal a pain we will not give to Him. One way to deal with our hurt is to imagine carrying all that pain and laying it at the feet of Christ. He welcomes our dependence on Him to restore our hearts and to handle our problems for us.

What's next? Lick your wounds. Lean into the lessons. The faster the better! Head up—wings out! And watch what God can do with your life.

"You'll never be able to grow if you're afraid to lose people during the process. Sometimes past relationships don't belong in new seasons."
~Trent Trenton

Pick Up Your Sword:

1. "Praise to the God of all comfort: Praise be to the God and Father of our Lord Jesus Christ, The Father of compassion and the God of all comfort, who comforts us in all our troubles, so that we can comfort those in any trouble with the comfort we ourselves receive from God."
   ~2 Corinthians 1:3-4 (NIV)
   What does this verse say to you about turning over your cares?

   _____

   _____

   _____

2. *"The steps of a good man are ordered by the Lord: and he delights in His ways."* ~ Psalm 37:23
   Your thoughts:

   _____

   _____

   _____

3. Steps for moving forward through the pain:
   a. Observe or recognize –was the offense intentional or a misunderstanding. Acknowledge what you are feeling. Remember that people who hurt people are hurting. Trust your heart when it tells you what happened. Determine you will respond rather than react.
   b. Don't defend yourself. Asking questions is always better than accusing the offending person. Avoid insisting on being right. Consider how you may have contributed to the situation. Seek to clarify the conflict with the goal of resolving.

c. Remind yourself that building bridges is to your advantage. Keep your personal boundaries, but always seek to forgive or ask for forgiveness. Where you can, extend kindness. You do not have to be a bashing post for the other person, but you do need to step back from being negative. Do your best to resolve what you can.

d. Walk away, pray, do positive self-care. Lick your wounds, sleep on it, and move on.

4. What's your plan for resolving conflict that hurts?

_____

_____

_____

5. Which of the three areas of growth need improvement? (Spiritual, physical, mental). Define how you plan to move forward.

_____

_____

_____

Audrey Hepburn, (1929-1993),

https://www.biography.com/actor/audrey-hepburn

one of the most beautiful women in the world said about being beautiful, "For beautiful eyes, look for the good in others; for beautiful lips, speak only words of kindness' and for poise, walk with the knowledge that you are never alone." An actress and humanitarian, she is remembered often for being one of Hollywood's greatest style icons.

Badassness! Stop doubting your greatness!

Always remember you are braver than you believe,
stronger than you seem,
and smarter than you think.
~Christopher Robin

Do you feel like you are going through the motions of life? Do you live for vacations or those occasional moments when all the stars align, and you feel awesome? Do you spend time in the 'what if' thoughts of dreams?

Life is not always about earning millions of dollars or becoming the next super star. More often life is about learning to be your true self, finding your purpose, and passing on the lesson. Your mission in life may be to support an elderly neighbor or teach a child to read.

There comes a time when we all need to stop wishing our lives away. We need to decide that we are going to take the step that will set our feet on the path of intentional living regardless of where it leads us. When we wish for a better life, without taking action, we may look up one day and thirty years have gone by. When we make a decision that says we are not looking back, every step moves us down the path.

It takes courage to turn your life upside-down and strike out on a path that perhaps takes more faith than you have ever attempted before. There will be knowns, and unknowns, but the simple fact that you are reading this says staying where you are is no longer an option for you. Your heart is already telling you there is more out there. You will never be content again until you try. You will have to deal with fears head on, some you'll win right away, and some will take many tries to conquer or manage. You will have to press forward and LET GO of self-limiting ideas.

We all make rules to govern our lives. Some rules are protective, and other rules have been handed down to us. Some boundaries we should keep. Some rules have outlived their usefulness. Some rules were created out of fear. Perhaps it is time to revisit the why of restrictions and decide if they hold us back or propel us forward. It is time to challenge our thinking, put away restrictive thinking and dare to be all that we are designed to be.

There comes a moment in time where staying where you are, is more painful than taking the risk to move on into unfamiliar territory.

Dr. Phil says, "If you always do what you've always done, you'll always get what you've always got."

The world needs people with visons brave enough to turn them from dreams to reality. The next generation needs pillars they can lean on to dream their dreams. If not us, then who? Those coming up through the ranks will find a leader to follow, do not miss the opportunity to be a quality example for their sake.

Pick Up Your Sword:

1. *"For I know the plans I have for you," declares the Lord, "plans to prosper you and not to harm you, plans to give you hope and a future."*
   ~ Jeremiah 29:11
   According to Jeremiah 29:11, why shouldn't we embrace our Badassness?

   _____

   _____

   _____

2. *"Accept who you are; and revel in it." ~ Mitch Albom* (Tuesdays with Morrie)
   What do you need to accept about yourself to be able to revel in it?

   _____

   _____

   _____

3. *"Never dull your shine for somebody else." ~ Tyra Banks*
   Your thoughts:

   _____

   _____

   _____

The first female prime minister of Britain. During her three terms, she cut social welfare programs, privatized certain industries, and reduced trade union power. Known as the 'Iron Lady', she held office during Britain's recession and bucked traditional 'policies.' One of her staunchest allies was President Ronald Regan.

Lesson 35

Challenge your thinking

"… but one thing I do, forgetting those things which are behind
and reaching forward to those things which are ahead,
14 I press toward the goal for the prize of the upward call
of God in Christ Jesus."
~ Philippians 3:13-14 KJV

We will have to stretch ourselves, our ideas, our self-limiting roles of who we are to embark on broadening ourselves. It is a bit annoying when strangers offer unsolicited commentaries. When those you are the closest to resist your changes or worse yet hold you to a personality profile from the past, their remarks can feel like shooting torpedo holes in your ship.

We could spend a lot of time trying to figure out where our self-limiting beliefs come from. We could waste life trying to find someone to blame. What if we instead act on the wisdom of the verse that says, "forgetting those things that were, press on to the higher calling of Christ." (Philippians 3:14)

Should we know where some of those false and damaging beliefs come from? Yes, do whatever you have to do to acknowledge them through adult eyes, deal with them, and then move on. I am not suggesting that we pretend pain is not painful, but I am suggesting that we not give these negative events any more power to deter us from being our best. Sometimes when we hang on to a painful event, we trap ourselves into continuing the abuse where the perpetrator left off. Allowing Christ to be our defender and healer, we can move through pain and onto our new path.

Maybe you do not have a painful past, you instead live in limbo like a wave on the sand, simply surviving life. Christ did not create us to live this way either. He clearly states, "I came that you might have life and have it abundantly" (John 10:10)

When others resist your new commitment to live life intentionally and to the fullest, realize that you may be touching their 'safe rules' and challenging their thinking. Perhaps they have not come to realize that they are living less than their best causing them to cling to their rules like a life raft in a turbulent ocean. The best way to quiet the criticism is to confidently go about improving you and daily reminding yourself that you serve an audience of one and He knows.

Pick Up Your Sword:

One of the steps to challenging your thinking is to follow the thought to its core.

Ask Why and What if?

For example:

1. I don't like doctor visits. Why?

2. Because every time I've taken someone to the doctor, it's bad news. Why?

3. I'm afraid they'll find something bad. Why?

4. I'm overweight and know better. Why?

5. I prefer to 'allow' myself this one flaw. Why?

6. I don't have time to take care of me while I'm taking care of everyone else.

What if?

1. What if I decide that I'm worthy of being taken care of so that I can take care of others?

2. What if they learn by example rather than words?

3. What if I take back my power and get healthy?

4. Perhaps these steps will end my fear-based visits to the doctor. Then give myself credit for being capable enough to handle whatever comes at me…I've proven it in the past, why wouldn't I do it again?

Do you see how finding the core of the problem can help you move toward the solution?

1. Now you try. List your Why's and What if's:

_____

_____

_____

_____

_____

2. What restraints hold you back? Follow them and take your power back.

_____

_____

_____

_____

_____

a hairdresser by trade, she introduced the first synthetic hairbrush in 1898. This innovative idea allowed brushing long hair more hygienic than the previous boar's hairbrushes. A futuristic innovator but also a woman's suffrage pioneer.

How is your view of you?

"Talk to yourself like you would to someone you love."
~*Brene Brown*

There is a saying that reminds us 'We are most like the five people we spend the bulk of our time with.' When I heard this, I had to think about my circle of influence and ask myself: Are they positive? Supportive? Able to challenge me or do they hold me where I am?

I have a coach that once said to me during a struggle, "The problem is you're trying to soar with eagles and you're swimming in a duck pond. Perhaps it's time to shoo the ducks and take flight." Take an inventory of where you are and where you want to be and look for opportunities to challenge yourself.

The Hard Work

God cannot direct a ship that is sitting still so part of moving forward is allowing fear to be mastered by faith. Andre Gide, a French author once said, "One does not discover new lands without consenting to lose sight of the shore." You are heading on an adventure; it means considering looking at our lives from a new perspective. That can be scary, but it can also be exhilarating.

One of the next steps is to make each thought answer to itself. We often spend more time playing loops in our head circling around the monster of 'What if?'

This is about maturing and resting in your faith. When your faith is bigger than your fears, you will move forward.

We spend more time worrying about the size of our thighs, the balance of our bank accounts, our cell phone version, our social media posts, and the color of our hair than we do about living our truest version of ourselves. When we get tangled in the perceived drama of our lives, we may miss the moments, right in front of us.

Several mantras remind us to live today:

- Be present, not perfect.
- Be mindful of little things.
- Respond rather than react.
- Proceed as if success is inevitable.

- Life/work balance rather than work/life balance
- Connections over things
- Experiences over stuff

With these thoughts of inspiration how do we move from where we are today to where we want to be tomorrow? Everyone needs goals or we can become complacent and drift into day-to-day mediocracy.

Start asking "What do I want?" and be specific. Using the **S.M.A.R.T** technique can help set goals. Each letter stands for a tool to use:

Specific – narrow down your goals so you know exactly what you want.

Measurable – define how you will know you attained your goal.

Attainable – is this goal realistic and achievable.

Relevant – is what you want aligned with who you are.

Time – set a reasonable date to attain the goal.

In the back of my planner, I keep goals for: physical, mental, spiritual, financial, travel and personal goals. I set goals for the month, the year, 5 years from now and 10 years from now. Then I love going back and checking them off. Having written goals makes them more realistic and keeps them in the forefront of thinking.

Pick Up Your Sword:

Take time to sit with yourself and write down your goals for:

1. Physical health:

   _____

   _____

   _____

2. Self-care:

   _____

   _____

   _____

3. Spiritual growth:

   _____

   _____

   _____

4. Financial goals:

   _____

   _____

   _____

5. Travel goals:

_____

_____

_____

6. Personal goals:

_____

_____

_____

Now go back and set timelines to meet these goals.

tirelessly committed her life to the better treatment of chimpanzees. She studied, lived with, and documented the life of chimps in the wild from 1970-1990. From an early age, fascinated by animal behavior, she developed a non-threatening means of observation and opened the eyes of the world to the gentle giants.

Frustration and Discouragement

"If you're going through hell, keep going!"
~Winston Churchill

The moment we start to move toward our goals and self-improvements, we will be scrutinized by those that are frustrated with their own lives. When we chose to stop sleeping through our life, we will threaten those that are snoring through their lives. Often the people we are closest to will be our worst critics.

Each time we start to talk about our new ideas, business, fitness, goals, or plans, we will feel the criticism in forms as minute as a chortle or an eye-roll. It wears on us, but now that we know it is coming, we can plan for it. Practice our sales pitch with a few pre-planned responses.

- Things are going great, why do you ask?

- Not everything is roses, but I am working in the garden.

- I am excited about the new things I am learning, thank you for asking.

When times get rough (which they will) and everyone questions your sanity, stay the fight. There will come a moment where you will hit a rhythm, or a pace and you will look into the face of success and recognize your own destiny and greatness!

I keep a magnet on my office wall that says: "Work as if success is eminent." Try keeping a musical play list of motivational music. I love "Fight Song" by Rachel Platten.

Pick Up Your Sword:

What do these verses say about our strength?

1. *"So do not fear, for I am with you; do not be dismayed, for I am your God. I will strengthen you and help you; I will uphold you with my righteous right hand." ~Isaiah 41:10*

_____

_____

2. "The Lord is my strength and my song; he has given me victory."
   ~ Exodus 15:2

   _____

   _____

3. *"Be strong and courageous; do not be frightened and do not be dismayed, for the Lord your God is with you wherever you go." ~ Joshua 1:9*

   _____

   _____

4. *"He gives power to the weak and strength to the powerless." ~ Isaiah 40:29*

   _____

   _____

5. *"My flesh and my heart may fail, but God is the strength of my heart and my portion forever." ~ Psalm 73:26*

   _____

   _____

6. *"I can do all this through him who gives me strength." ~ Philippians 4:13*

   _____

   _____

7. *"The Lord is my strength; he makes my feet like the feet of a deer; he enables me to tread on the heights." ~ Habakkuk 3:19*

   _____

   _____

8. *"The Lord gives strength to his people; the Lord blesses his people with peace." ~ Psalm 29:11*

   _____

   _____

9. *"But those who hope in the Lord will renew their strength. They will soar on wings like eagles; they will run and not grow weary; they will walk and not be faint." ~ Isaiah 40:31*

   _____

   _____

Susan B. Anthony, (1820-1906),

https://www.britannica.com/biography/Susan-B-Anthony

a tireless women's rights pioneer. Her work paved the way for giving women the right to vote. A target of newspaper abuse and public criticism she stood her ground for women's rights. During the Civil War she helped organize the Women's National Loyal League urging for emancipation. As chief New York agent of Garrison's American Anti-Slavery Society for all rights. She is honored on the 1979 Susan B. Anthony silver dollar.

Lesson 38

Picking Your Forever Partner

"I guarantee there will be tough times.
I guarantee at some point one or both of us
are going to want to get out of this thing.
But I also guarantee if I don't ask you to be mine,
I'll regret it for the rest of my life
because I know, in my heart you're the only one for me."
~Runaway Bride Movie 1999

Falling in love verses staying in love has its blessings and work. Falling in love has all the warm fuzzies, fireworks and anticipation of romantic interludes for the rest of our lives. Many of us were raised on Disney movies that make 'happily ever after' look so easy. Never will we be involved in a relationship that will require more of our best selves than with a life partner. And in a country where statistics scream that 50% of marriages will fail, we better have a strategy to help eliminate the heartache of tearing apart a till death do us part commitment. There is a saying, "The only thing perfect about marriage is the airbrushed wedding photo." ~Anonymous. If that is the truth than how can we prevent failure and prepare for success?

The first step is knowing who we are and what we value. Family, faith, career, friends, common likes, values, future goals all come in to play when considering a life linked together. Ask yourself what matters to you in each category. What does it look like for you this year, next year and subsequent years down the road? Make a 'Who I am' list:

Who I am:

Family: _____

Faith: _____

Career: _____

Friends: _____

Hobbies: _____

Activities: _____

Pets: _____

Health: _____

Income: _____

Decide what you like and do not like in each category and what would be a deal breaker.

For example: If you are a health nut, and are active as a rule, will you be okay with someone who lives on fast food and prefers gaming all weekend on the couch? Be as descriptive as you can be for each topic. Then make a list of what you are looking for in a partner. This will be a 'I want':

I want in a partner:

Start with your I am list and then add other items on your list to be watching for:

Family oriented: _____

Good with kids:_____

Loyal: _____

Patient:_____

Security:_____

Easy personality: _____

Make your list long and detailed. Then write beside each item how you will determine that they meet or come up short for each item that you value.

Once you have written down what you are looking for in a partner, start prayerfully looking. Do not share the list with anyone else but be observant with each potential. If you are dating, this is a quick way to determine if the date is a potential mate or just for fun. Dating can be a great process of discovering prospective spouses, but it can also be valuable to defining reasons to move on. Marriage is a long-term process. Moving slow is the optimum speed. You will want to see your potential mate in good times and tough situations. Go through the holidays to see if their values line up with yours. You will want to know when the tough stuff of life is thrown at them, how they react or respond.

Bringing Christ into your choices is the most valuable culling practice you can bring to the process. Since God created us, He knows best who can weather the sunshine and storms of a life spent together. Ask Him. Then be willing to hear the answer.

Pick Up Your Sword:

1. *"Love is patient and kind; love does not envy or boast; it is not arrogant or rude. It does not insist on its own way; it is not irritable or resentful; it does not rejoice at wrongdoing but rejoices with the truth. Love bears all things, believes all things, hopes all things, endures all things."*
    ~ 1 Corinthians 13:4-7
    How can you choose a partner that demonstrates these attributes?

    _____

    _____

    _____

2. *"He who finds a wife finds a good thing and obtains favor from the Lord."*
    ~ Proverbs 18:22
    What makes a good wife?

    _____

    _____

    _____

3. *"Do not be unequally yoked with unbelievers. For what partnership has righteousness with lawlessness? Or what fellowship has light with darkness? "*
    ~ 2 Corinthians 6:14
    What does this verse caution against for partnerships?

    _____

    _____

    _____

4. *"Above all, keep loving one another earnestly, since love covers a multitude of sins." ~ 1 Peter 4:8*
    Your thoughts?

    _____

    _____

    _____

5. *"Let all that you do be done in love." ~ 1 Corinthians 16:14*
    Do you see this in yourself? In your future mate?

    _____

    _____

    _____

6. *"And we know that in all things God works for the good of those who love him, who have been called according to his purpose."* ~ Romans 8:28
Is your relationship called according to His purpose?

_____

_____

_____

Rahab was a prostitute in the city of Jericho. When the Hebrews began to conquer Canaan, Rahab harbored their spies in her house in exchange for her family's safety. Rahab recognized the True God. After the walls of Jericho fell, the Israelite army kept their promise, protecting Rahab's house.

Rahab became the ancestress of King David, and from David's line came Jesus Christ, the Messiah. Rahab played a key role in God's plan of salvation for the world.

Secrets to Sticking and Staying Married

*"Falling in love and having a relationship
are two different things."*
~Keanu Reeves

The death rate of marriages is far greater than twenty years ago, why is that? It seems it is a rarity to see couples who have been married twenty plus years and yet it still strikes a heart-chord when we see couples up in years walking together holding hands.

It does not take long to determine who is dating and who is settled too far into the comfort zone of married life. Next time you are in a restaurant, observe the couples around you. Are they talking? Holding hands? Or are they engrossed in their phones, the paper, or simply eating without even looking at one another?

Truth is marriage is one of the most rewarding relationships but is also the hardest undertaking engaged in as well. It takes daily, constant care to stick and stay together. There are often great sacrifices necessary to create a harmony or team spirit. And the daily skirmishes must be weighed out based on priority and importance. One of the tougher skills to staying married is overlooking faults, mistakes, and just plain annoyances.

Here are a few secrets that might help our relationship longevity:

Don't lose the flirt:

Good sexy flirting with your spouse reminds the other that they are at the forefront of your thinking. It's like the seasoning on a good taco. The taco is nutritional by itself, but the hot sauce adds the zesty flavor and extra enjoyment. Sexy verbal texts, good grooming, and even pizza by candlelight can be sexy.

Shower together:

Create your own little world away from the rest of the universe even if for only ten minutes. Generally, lives pull us in two different directions all day long. Starting the day together allows a check in with one another. And a few moments of skin-to-skin contact can make all the difference in the world. In the real world, often the joy of making love can be relegated to once a week, so ten minutes in the shower to just reconnect is a valuable asset.

Teamwork:

Understanding each other's strengths and weaknesses will better build a team that provides a well-oiled problem-solving machine when crisis's hit—and we all know the crisis will hit sooner or later. A partner you can count on with their unique skills can make a successful alliance. There is nothing harder on a marriage than having one of the partners discount the other. For the disregarded spouse, it's like being a world class athlete drafted to the big leagues and then benched because the coach does not recognize their ability to perform. Take the time to observe the strengths in your spouse.

Date:

There is nothing harder on a relationship than when it becomes all about survival and work. If your job takes all your time, stay single. If you are married strive to perfect balance in a chaotic world, by finding moments of fun and intimacy. If you have children, employ grandma, trade with a friend, or hire a sitter on a regular basis. It is possible to carve out time, even if it is minutes; people make time for what is important to them and our spouses know that. Let go of the idea of only reconnecting on vacation or a twice a year extravagant date. Do not lose those ideas but realize that breakfast once a week, a short drive, or a soak in the tub for twenty minutes can be just as invigorating to the psyche of a relationship.

Little Things Matter:

Please, thank you, I love you, I appreciate you, and how'd I get so lucky? All these little things matter. Write them on a note, text them, leave a card, on the bathroom mirror. Find twenty ways to say I love you or you mean the world to me and say them often. Do a chore that is typically the other person's job without saying a word. Leave a voice mail message listing five things that you admire about your significant other. Praise them for doing the day-to-day mundane tasks they do to keep the team afloat.

Breakfast Business Meetings:

When schedules and events over-run our lives, take time away from the hustle and bustle and hold planning meetings. Bring your calendar, ideas, and issues to discuss on a list already established in priorities. Then stick to the topics, jointly decide what goes, what stays, and strategize a plan of attack. Leave the emotions behind by considering this a business strategy meeting. If you come to an impasse, the person that cares the most carries more weight in the decision or voting process.

Laugh Together:

Do not take yourself too seriously. Learn each other's sense of humor. Remember for jokes to be funny, laugh together at something, not at the other person's expense. Explore doing things that the other person likes and find common ground that both of you can do together.

Be open, vulnerable, and try to see things from the other person's perspective.

Think before you speak and respond before you react. Do not hold grudges and get to forgiveness quicker. If you can do these things, you will be that elderly couple still holding hands celebrating 50 years of togetherness.

25 Ways lovers say I Love You!

In this world of moving at the speed of sound, we need to remind our heartbeats that they are on the top of our list even if we have to fight to find time for them. These 25 tips will keep them smiling and thrilled that they matter to you. Use today's technology to help you express your feelings!

1. I love the way you laugh from your toes.
2. I smile every time I see you coming.
3. My day is always brighter when we spend time together.
4. I know you hate going to work but thank you for providing for us.
5. You are the best thing that has happened to me in my life.
6. Leave notes in random places for them to find.
7. Find heart stickers and stick them all over the inside of their car.
8. Text a heart and thumbs up consistently. If you know their day is a tough one,   and you have done it enough times, text it for a smile on their day.
9. Leave your song on their voice mail.
10. Leave their favorite dessert somewhere random.
11. If you are going to be gone, slip a card under their pillow so they will find it later.
12. Write on a card one special memory for every year you have been together that happened during that year. It takes effort, but that is what makes it special.
13. Clean the inside of their car when they least expect it.
14. Discover their love language and love them that way.

15. Leave a sexy note where you know they will find it.

16. Leave a trail of clothing to your room.

17. Light candles or those battery-operated ones all over the living room and spread a blanket on the floor for an indoor picnic.

18. Dance to your song in the kitchen every morning while waiting for the coffee. Think of the lovely memory that will bring every time they hear it.

19. Call their voicemail and leave a sexy description of what is waiting for them later. This brings all day anticipation.

20. Plan a sunrise hot coffee/chocolate date just to be alone for 15 minutes quietly watching the morning arrive.

21. A midnight date to a 24-hour drive through for a hotdog keeps things spontaneous. (We love Sonic or Krispy Kreme donuts)

22. Make up and leave a certificate of appreciation on the refrigerator for them to find.

23. Do a chore for them that they usually do and/or hate.

24. Wear something sexy (or nothing) under your sweats that only they know about while you do random chores.

25. Have one piece of clothing that indicates you want body to body time with them, so there is no guessing. You can also wear this item at a dinner even if others are around. I have a specific dress; my guy has a certain shirt. We know what it means, and the anticipation and flirting fill the evening.

Until you build your own 25 list, use this one. The only rule is to make your significant other feel significant.

Pick up your sword:

1. Make your own 25 list:

   _____

2. What areas of your relationship can you improve on?

   _____

   _____

   _____

3. List 3 unique but special dates you can create:

   _____

   _____

   _____

Maya Angelou, (1928-2014),

https://www.biography.com/writer/maya-angelou

American poet, singer, actress, dancer, and civil rights activist. Raped at the age of seven, her uncles killed the perpetrator. As an African American woman, she lived daily with racial prejudices and discrimination. Raised by her grandmother in Arkansas, her experiences turned her into an advocate for peace. Her autobiographical work, 'I Know Why the Caged Bird Sings' gained critical acclaim.

Falling in Love or Staying in Love

"A successful marriage requires falling in love many times,
always with the same person."
~Mignon McLaughlin

I was an impressionable teen in the 70s. My head was filled with Romeo and Juliet (1968 with Olivia Hussey), Love Story (1970, Ryan O'Neil and Ali McGraw), Camelot (1967, Richard Harris and Vanessa Redgrave), The Way We Were (1975, Robert Redford and Barbara Streisand), and Grease (1978, Olivia Newton John and John Travolta). I had the feeling love was something that floated down from the sky and landed on you with a profound assurance it had found you and the journey was over.

It's not on the one, it's not the mambo. It's a feeling; a heartbeat.
{ Johnny to Baby from Dirty Dancing }

I soon learned how naïve those thoughts really were. Falling in love is only the beginning. Staying in love is a whole different story. So, when that singular and grand love everyone dreams about did find me, I was surprised to find the journey was far from over. Throughout the years it has taken a lot of care to keep our love healthy and growing. Like a garden there is a lot of tending to be done. She taught me just the right lessons to help pull the weeds out of our relationship.

Ten important things my garden taught me about love:

Water often and deeply: Love needs to grow deep roots to avoid surface growth that can burn out easily. Love is hydrated with daily praise. Take the time to notice and compliment character traits you admire.

Beauty Fades: Over time beauty fades like the blossom of a rose, but the fragrance lingers. Give compliments and show admiration for things that will not fade in time. Appreciate your lover's ability to solve problems, and to maintain patience with a fussy baby, a troubled teen, or a sensitive child. Applaud their efforts to stay the course when others might not. If properly cultured, love grows, and the bloom will leave its fragrance on the cultivator. So, it may be with relationships that are tenderly developed.

Safeguard Consistently: It's essential to protect the garden from enemies. Left unprotected, plants and relationships can be easily destroyed. Daily, pull out the weeds when they are little, and their roots aren't as capable of destroying the main stalk. Speaking up in a relationship when strains are first discovered can create a perseverant partnership. Even seasoned growth needs boundaries and proper reinforcement. Consider the slug. His single-purposed is to devour everything in its path. Don't think he will go after the weeds. He prefers the best the garden has to offer. If allowed to run free, destruction is certain. Safeguarding love means keeping the slugs out of the garden to assure continued growth. Building boundaries safeguards longevity.

Beauty is in the eye of the beholder: Every gardener has their favorite flower for whatever reasons each one has. My friend loves lilies, and I cannot stand the smell of them. I adore Lavender and my husband always asks, "What stinks?" Behaviors and traits of our spouses come with spectator choices. We can either classify the habit as an endearment or an irritant. Be slow to decide the flower's fate or the habits' providence.

A time for everything: Plants need a time to grow, a time to flourish and a time to rest. Relationships need quality and quantity of time, likewise relationships also need time alone, a personal quiet time to internally grow.

Pay attention: Do not be afraid to change the climate for a plant that isn't doing well. It might need more watering, fertilizer, or re-fortified soil to inspire growth. Rookie plants can often survive on extraordinarily little, but once established the needs of the mature plant change; the gardener must adapt to the advanced needs of the older growth. To neglect the adult requirements could mean the death of a favorite bloomer.

Two can be better than one: When grafting a cutting into an established host, the hope is that the two will become one. If the cutting is rejected, its removal can cause the death of both grafted pieces. Choose carefully; once merged together, a pulling apart can harm even the strongest stalk. If the merge is successful, the new plant will be stronger than originally creating a partnership that will stand the test of storms and time.

Select Carefully: Some plants are showstoppers, and some are supporting stage setters. Blend together carefully. I at times planted two showstoppers side by side only to have them compete until I moved one of them. It was only once I relocated one of them that they both became all they could be. People can be like that; know yourself well enough to find someone who compliments you rather than competes with you.

Old gardens are beautiful: New gardens along with the anticipation of creating a garden, brings out an excitement and passion in the gardener. But it is the established garden that brings the surety of spring following winter. The long-established garden, though toilsome at first to create, self-perpetuates continued growth and beauty with much less effort. The roots are deep and much more able to sustain themselves during difficult times. Staying in love, once the hard work is completed, also perpetuates a staying power that new love has not yet discovered. Although zeal and passion motivate new relationships, devotion, dedication, and commitment build the staying power for the journey.

Celebrate the Beauty: Take time to enjoy the nuances of the garden. Do not forget the little things individually and collectively that consistently perpetuate the garden to be its best. Frame the garden in the best possible manner you are capable of. Speak of the beauty of your garden often. Remember you are responsible for being its ambassador. Sometimes you are the only way spectators may see the garden. How you tend the garden may inspire others to create their own strong relationships.

When I was young, I believed love just happened and that I had no control of falling in or falling out of love. As the years have marched on by, I have learned that love happens intentionally. The staying power of love is based in knowing who I am through the creator of ultimate love. As I learn to embrace an unconditional love built on the steadfastness of the rock of Christ, I have learned to love myself in a way that allows me to give love away. This gift of love is like dropping a rock in a lake, the ripples reflect love's natural outward movement. I never know where the ripples will end up and I guess I do not have to know; it is enough that the movement extends outward rather than inward--- demonstrating the power of "falling in" versus "staying in".

Pick Up Your Sword:

1.   *"Above all, love each other deeply, because love covers a multitude of sins."*
     ~ 1 Peter 4:8
     According to this verse how are we to love one another?

     _____

     _____

     _____

2. *"Though one may be overpowered, two can defend themselves. A cord of three strands is not quickly broken." ~ Ecclesiastes 4:12 (NIV)*
If a marriage is of two people, who is the third strand?

_____

_____

_____

3. *"Be completely humble and gentle; be patient, bearing with one another in love." ~ Ephesians 4:2 (NIV)*
How are we to love each other?

_____

_____

_____

4. *"Put on then, as God's chosen ones, holy and beloved, compassionate hearts, kindness, humility, meekness, and patience, bearing with one another and, if one has a complaint against another, forgiving each other' as the Lord has forgiven you, so you also must forgive. And above all these put on love, which binds everything together in perfect harmony."*
~ Colossians 3:12-14 (ESV)
If we have a fight our spouse, how are we to handle it?

_____

_____

_____

5. *"He who finds a wife finds a good thing and obtains favor from the Lord."*
~ Proverbs 18:22
As women, why should we strive to be a 'good' wife?

_____

_____

6. *"This is my commandment, that you love one another as I have loved you."*
~ John 15:12
We have been called to demonstrate the highest level of love. What should that look like in our marriage?

_____

_____

Ruth was a virtuous young widow, so upright in character that her love story is one of the favorite accounts in the entire Bible. When her Jewish mother-in-law Naomi returned to Israel from Moab after a famine, Ruth pledged to follow Naomi and worship her God.

Boaz exercised his right as kinsman-redeemer, married Ruth, and rescued both women from poverty. According to Matthew, Ruth was an ancestor of King David, whose descendant was Jesus Christ.

Invest Wisely in Friendships

> *"Each friend represents a world in us,*
> *a world possibly not born until they arrive,*
> *and it is only by this meeting that a new world is born."*
> *~ Anais Nin*

I've Got Your Back! —Investing Wisely in Friendships

Friendships are vital to our physical and spiritual health. They bring quality to our lives. Choosing a good friendship is an opportunity to learn about ourselves, to grow as a person, and to embrace the abundance in life. A good friend reminds us of our great qualities and calls us out when we are heading toward destruction.

A friend sees our faults but can also see beyond them and encourages us to stretch ourselves. A friend celebrates success with you and hands you chocolate during the tough times! Friendships increase your sense of belonging and inspires to pursue our purposes. In the story of David and Johnathon, they are called Ranger buddies. They were committed friends for life. They looked out for each other.

Ever wonder where the saying, "I've got your back," came from? Soldiers who fought with swords to protect themselves and each other literally fought back-to-back. They were assured of never being stabbed in the back because of this fighting strategy.

This kind of friendship will stand the test of time. You need someone equal in strength to you. Not necessarily the same strengths, skills, or gifting, but someone who can hold up their end when you need it. You want someone who will cheerlead when you need it and someone who will call you out when you are off course. You will need a friend who you can be completely transparent with and who is wise enough not to hate your family when you complain about them.

The relationship should be equal, you are there for them as much as they are there for you. The equality of the strength in the friendship is vital or it might become a mentoring situation. Learn to pray with and for them. Respect their other relationships by knowing your place in their lives but be bold enough to challenge them to be their best and accept that challenge from them.

Deborah and Jael's story: Judges 4 & 5

Deborah was a judge in her community, a strong leader. She is known for her wisdom and for hearing from God. She sought his wisdom daily. She was the only woman identified as a judge in scriptures.

Deborah's name means flames or a woman of torches. This referred to being someone who illuminated the way for others. She was the wife of Lappidoth. She sat under a palm tree between the towns of Ramah and Bethel in the hills of Ephraim. The Israelites would come to her to settle arguments. She was looked to for leadership in the land. Barak, Abinoam's son, held her in high regard and respected her judgement.

Barak shared with Deborah he had been commanded by God to take 10,000 men to defeat Jabin's large army. When Barak did not engage, Deborah called him out and asked why he was not doing what God had told him to do.

Barak said, "If you go with me, I'll go. But if you will not, I'm not going."

Deborah said, "I'll go with you, but you will not get the credit. The Lord will hand over Sisera (the commander) to a woman."

Together they went to Kedesh and defeated Jabin's army. There were no survivors except for one: Sisera, the commander of the armies. Deborah was celebrating her win over Jabin's army while Barak continued to chase Sisera through the country. Following this victory, she drove her chariot home I am sure to shower and relax. Imagine for a moment, the extent of her confidence to lead an army to war, fight with them and then drive herself home. Managing the chariot might be more than most of us could handle but she did it following an extended time of physical battle. I am impressed!

Sisera, seeing the battle was lost, got off his chariot and fled on foot. His escape took him to the home of Jael, the wife of Heber, the Kenite and good friend to Deborah. There was a peace treaty between Heber, and King Jabin, so Sisera felt safe asking for refuge from Jael.

At the mercy of a political alliance that kept her from being part of the Israelite community, she was caught in the middle. Knowing who he was, and supportive or Deborah's battle, she invited Sisera in to eat and rest. Jael filled his belly with stew and suggested he sleep. She said she would stand at the door of the tent so no one would bother him.

Jael knew Deborah was at war. Should she protect Sisera or protect her alliance with Deborah and the Israelites? Decisively, she made her choice and drove a tent stake through the commander's head, nailing it to the ground while he slept. She was a woman of action. Jael had in a single blow killed the leader of the army. Imagine her confidence and fitness to complete this task. She had one shot and must have lifted the mallet with one hand while she held the tent stake hovering over Sisera's head. The story tells us she hit him so hard she drove the tent stake through his head and into the ground on the other side. Shortly after, Barak arrived still chasing Sisera. Jael said, "Come and I'll show you the man you're after." There he found Sisera dead.

Jael and Deborah are credited with 40 years of peace in the land following these events. Both women displayed great courage and physical strength!

Lessons we can learn:

Friendship: Besides listening/obeying God and being incredibly physically fit, they teach us about devoted friendship—a warrior friendship.

Too often, strong women are drawn to mentoring relationships. There is nothing wrong with mentoring—in fact, we are called in Titus 2 to be mentors. But we need to cultivate the kind of friendship that is a Warrior Friendship.

Leadership: If you are called to be a leader, then lead. If you do not lead, battles will be lost that should have been won.

Be You: Society often has set images of who we should be. Swim upstream! Sometimes going against societal expectations is necessary to be who you are designed to be.

Choose Friends Carefully: they may be the only thing between you and a sword! Know where your allegiances lie.

Pick Up Your Sword:

1. *"Oil and perfume make the heart glad; So, does the sweetness of a friend's counsel that comes from the heart." ~ Proverbs 27:9*
   What does this verse say about friends?

   _____

   _____

   _____

2. *"For we are God's handiwork, created in Christ Jesus to do good works, which God prepared in advance for us to do." ~ Ephesians 2:10*
   What does Ephesians 2:10 say about who you are?

   _____

   _____

   _____

3. *"A person of too many friends comes to ruin, but there is a friend who sticks closer than a brother." ~ Proverbs 18:24*
   What does Proverbs 18:24 say about true friends?

   _____

   _____

   _____

4. *"A friend loves at all times, and a brother is born for adversity."*
    ~ Proverbs 17:17
    What does Proverbs 17:17 say about being a friend?

    _____

    _____

    _____

5. *"Some friends may ruin you. But a real friend will be more loyal than a*
    brother." ~ Proverbs 18:24
    Proverbs 18:24 is a friend warning. What is it?

    _____

    _____

    _____

6. We are influenced the most by the five people we spend time with besides
    our immediate family. With that in mind, are the people you hang-out with the
    best influences or do you need a change? Name them below and give them
    a 1–5-star rating. (1- not so good, 5- the best)

    _____

    _____

    _____

    _____

    _____

Ranger Buddy Tips:

- Pray for and with each other. Pray together for others.
- Meet often to set life goals and ask about them.
- Take time to play and have adventures, they bond friends.
- Celebrate success together!

"Why did you do all this for me?' he asked.
'I don't deserve it. I've never done anything for you.'
'You have been my friend,' replied Charlotte.
'That in itself is a tremendous thing."
— E.B. White, Charlotte's Web

an American poet, an introvert, spent years taking care of her sick mother and was treated for a painful eye ailment. She rarely left the confines of her homestead but produces some of her pest poetry during this time. Very few of her poems were published while she was alive, but her writings soared following her death.

Defining an admirable woman

"It's better to be thought a fool
than to open your mouth unbecomingly and remove all doubt."
~Abraham Lincoln

What makes an admirable woman? What are the traits of a woman worth admiring? There are as many variables of worthy characteristics as there are women. But there are some common qualities like a golden thread that distinguishes them. They know their true worth, who they are and what they stand for. They understand their strengths and weaknesses and continue to grow by challenging themselves. They understand that happiness comes from within not from circumstances around them.

Another characteristic of a woman worth admiring is a sense of mystery. They avoid being chatterboxes, which makes a person look desperate, self-focused or afraid to hear her own thoughts. Sometimes weak speaking habits can keep people from hearing you as a person. You can be judged too quickly and written off before you really get a chance.

Instead, we need to be slow to speak. I remember being in a group situation where one of the women only spoke up when she had some quality comment to add to the conversation, and I noticed the room quieted whenever she spoke up. That is an influencer.

Women of history have influenced great changes in our worlds. They stand up for what is right and for what they believe in. They have standards that set the bar for others to emulate. They are hard-working, witty, respectable, modest, humble, confident leaders. They keep their heads about them in a crisis, they refuse to let difficulties get them down permanently, their beauty comes from within, and they are courageous. They take ownership for themselves and are responsible. They are loyal and honest. They finish what they start and understand their limits and boundaries. They have good manners and yet know how to enjoy a good laugh. Their elegance commands a room.

Experiences trigger lessons to use along life's pathway. We cannot be all these things all at once. Becoming an admirable woman is a process. Making any change is tough, but changes allow the real you to be seen.

Pick Up Your Sword:

1. What women do you know that you admire?

   _____

   _____

   _____

2. Why? What qualities do you see in them as worthy to be admired?

   _____

   _____

   _____

3. What qualities do you want to work on?

   _____

   _____

   _____

Barbara Walters, (1921- present),

https://www.biography.com/media-figure/barbara-walters

broadcast journalist, author, and television personality. Known for being the first female co-anchor on NBC's Today show and ABC's 20/20. She traveled with First Lady Jacqueline Kennedy on a trip to India catapulting her career as a serious journalist. Her straight talk with those she interviewed built a signature style earning her many awards for best host in a talk series.

Just Living or Living Abundantly?

"To live abundantly, you have to race toward the future
with heart and arms wide open.
You have to risk everything and
let the universe take care of the details."
~Elaine Hussey

Sword or Shield? Living Life Offensively or Defensively? They both have their purpose, but if you spend all your time playing a game defensively, you will never score or win.

Football season happens every fall. Teams are stacked to their best positions to win the game. Winning teams need both the defensive team and the offensive team. The overarching goal of both teams is to win the game, but the defense is focused on stopping the opposing side's advances while the offense's purpose is to advance the ball down the field to score.

Like football, life too has its seasons. Sometimes we are building new beginnings deep in training and other times we're learning new skills to play the game of life better. Both have their places.

You can imagine the chaos that would occur if an offensive player ran out when the defensive team was on the field. The offensive player has been trained to score and may thwart the team's success at stopping the downfield movement by the other team. Likewise, if a defensive player only stopped the other team, they would not be in a position to advance the ball for a win.

Once we identify our personal gifting or purpose in life, we are ready to shift from the defensive stance to the offensive mode. As a Badass warrior, battles are won with shields lifted and feet pressing forward toward the goal. Our gifts, our talents, our wisdom were not given to us solely for our personal use. We are the curators of these gifts by design to share with others. If our talents are to be useful, it becomes necessary to make the most of both offensive and defensive modes. We must take purposeful strides forward to share and equip the other team players in our lives.

"People who live a life of purpose have core beliefs and values that influence their deci-sions, shape their day-to-day actions, and determine their short- and long-term priori-ties. They place significant value on being a person of high integrity and in earning the trust and respect of others. The result is that they live with a clear conscience and spend more time listening to their inner voice than being influenced by others."
~ Frank Sonneberg

Throwing our hands up, living on emotions, procrastinating, being unprepared are all defensive tools of sabotage that rob us from success.

What can we do today to embrace a winning lifestyle? Let's talk about Defensive moves to protect ourselves and Offensive moves to start winning the badass game.

Defensive moves:

- Setting good boundaries

- Stopping bad habits

- Stop blame shifting.

- Stop living in the past —or resolve it so you can move forward.

- Be aware of the opponents' strategies to counter them.

- Pay attention.

- Don't attack when fatigue dominates.

- Never react —always respond thoughtfully.

- Accurately assess the situation

- Be aware of the battlefield and the true costs.

Offensive moves:

- Define your values, present, and future and set goals.

- Prioritize—Decide what matters most.

- Have a plan to get from here to 'there'.

- Work the plan—you would be surprised how many don't.

- Recognize when you get off-track—have an accountability coach.

- When you get off track, get back as quick as possible.

- Use resources—ask others what they see as strengths and weaknesses.

- Accept that failure is part of the process (get over being perfect)

- Keep your promises—strive to consistently build your reputation.

- Set boundaries and stick to them.

- Respect yourself enough to expect more of you and the people around you that don't treat you with value.
- Be present in your own life – stop wishing what it could be and evaluate honestly what it really is, then plan to do better based on your goals.
- Give back—the saying "Each one, teach one," is about learning the way to success and passing it on to someone else.

Take time to be still. Spend time alone—get to know you, then listen to the Father for direction. He wants you to live an abundant life—embrace it!

Mediocre People	Successful People
Inaction	Take action
Talk Orientated	Action orientated
Read negative news	Read success related news
Read negative newspapers	Read success magazines
Don't read books	Read success books
Listen to music	Listen to motivational/personal development videos
Play computer games	Take action
Discuss people	Discuss ideas
Watch excess amounts of TV	Take action
Sleep too much	Rest well
Wake up late	Wake up early
Small talk	Take action
Time wasting	Take action

Love entertainment	Love action and self-education
Procrastinating	Take action
No schedule	Clear schedule for their day
Lack of focus	Focused on success

Pick Up Your Sword:

1. Are you living your life offensively or defensively?

   _____

   _____

2. What kinds of things do you do that you consider defensive living?

   _____

   _____

3. What kinds of steps can you take to move from a defensive position in your life to a take-charge offensive kind of life?

   _____

   _____

4. What is the first change you can make today?

   _____

   _____

5. "Therefore, since we are surrounded by so great a cloud of witnesses, let us also lay aside every weight, and sin which clings so closely, and let us run with endurance the race that is set before us, looking to Jesus, the founder and perfecter of our faith, who for the joy that was set before him endured the cross, despising the shame, and is seated at the right hand of the throne of God." Just as Jesus patiently endured suffering, before he received the reward, we too must run with endurance." ~ Hebrews 12:1-2

   What does this verse say about becoming a forward moving warrior?

   _____

   _____

   _____

6. *Paul asks, "Do you not know that in a race all the runners run, but only one receives the prize? So run that you may obtain it." ~ 1 Corinthians 9:24*
Your thoughts:

_____

_____

_____

Dorothy Height, (1912-2010),

https://www.biography.com/activist/dorothy-height

called the godmother of the women's movement for her work for gender equality. A teacher, she worked with Eleanor Roosevelt and led the National Council of Negro Women, (NCNW) and the Young Women's Christian Association (YWCA) and received the Presidential Medal of Freedom. As a tireless activist she also established the Center for Racial Justice.

Defining Stewardship

"The first job of a leader, at home or at work,
is to inspire trust.
It's to bring out the best in people by
entrusting them with meaningful stewardships,
and to create an environment in which
high trust interaction inspires creativity and possibility."
~Stephen M.R. Covey

Stewardship. It's a funny word. Stewardship is the task of responsibly planning, caring for and management of people, resources, gifts, and talents. Any emergency (ice storms, fires, job loss, earthquakes, floods, pandemics) help to teach us that being prepared is an asset. For example, when the pandemic hit in 2020 and there was a toilet paper shortage, we were able to relax here in our home. We make it a habit to stock up on sale items and one of them was toilet paper. Equally when we were evacuated due to fires, we had back up funds to accommodate hotel and food needs. Our insurance covered our expenses but not immediately. I'm not sure what we would have done without the back-up emergency cash. We have a savings account that we place a few dollars in regularly and pretend it does not exist. After a length of time, we had acquired a healthy sum which covered the upfront cost of $2200 during our emergency stay. When the ice storms hit in 2021, we had plenty of backup foods in the pantry, wood for the woodstove, and batteries for the flashlights/lanterns. We are not rich, but we bought these things a little at a time and were prepared during emergencies. That's the core of stewardship— being wisely prepared.

Knowing what you need and finding ways to acquire them without breaking the bank can save your household and those around you. Some ways to save are below:

- Sewing
- Bargain hunting
- Garage sale
- Pantry foods (sale items for recipes)
- Couponing
- Gleaning
- Plan a month of meals.

- Cooking skills
- Meals that stretch the dollar
  https://homeschoolbasicsa-z.com/product/rookie-chefs-on-a-budget/
- Recipes that serve diet, budget and easy to make
  https://homeschoolbasicsa-z.com/product/rookie-chefs-on-a-budget/
- Second-hand store bargains
- Savings
- Home-based businesses
  https://homeschoolbasicsa-z.com/build-a-home-based-business/build-a-business-introduction/

Pick Up Your Sword:

1. *"She looks for wool and linen and works with her hands in delight. She is like merchant ships; she brings her food from afar." ~ Proverbs 31:13-14*
   How does the Proverbs woman in the verses above demonstrate stewardship?

   _____

   _____

   _____

2. *"She selects wool and flax and works with eager hands." ~ Proverbs 31:13*
   How can we provide clothing for our families like the Proverbs woman? (Sewing, 2nd hand stores, garage sales, hand-me-downs)

   _____

   _____

   _____

3. *"She is like the merchant ships, bringing her food from afar." ~ Proverbs 31:14*
   We do not have to travel far or wait for the merchant ships for our food, but what can we do to serve our families and be good stewards?

   _____

   _____

   _____

Harriet Tubman, (1822-1913),

https://www.biography.com/activist/harriet-tubman

Born a slave, she escaped and eventually returned to free her family. During the next twelve years she returned twenty times and each time helped other enslaved black people ushering them along the underground railroad—freeing over 300 people. During the Civil war she worked as a nurse, a scout, and a spy for the Union forces. After the war, she helped build schools for slaves.

Earning a Home-Based Income

"People are basically the same the world over.
Everybody wants the same things - to be happy,
to be healthy, to be at least reasonably prosperous,
and to be secure.
They want friends, peace of mind,
good family relationships,
and hope that tomorrow is going to be
even better than today."
~Zig Ziglar

As a multi-tasking warrior woman, influencer, and 'get-it-done' woman, there are strong reasons to build an income based from home. Anytime you can limit your commute time, meeting times, coffee networking times, clothing allowance, and eating out budget you're already ahead in the game. When I networked and worked away from home, I was extremely limited as to how many clients I could take on. Once I moved my business home and used zoom meetings, I was able to help triple the clients. Between meeting breaks, I can throw in a load of laundry, fill the crockpot for dinner, take a nap, walk the dog and water the garden. My overhead budget decreased substantially, and no one knows I'm wearing sweats and slippers from the waist down!

Once you've decided to base yourself or create a business from home, there are several items to consider:

Blending Business and Passion — There is a way to blend your passions into a business. Ask yourself 10 questions to help define your home-based income future! Watch this video to get you started. (https://daretobeabadass.com/blending-business-and-passion-part-1/)

Naming Your Business — What's in a name? There are some do's and don'ts. Choosing a business name should be unique but not difficult to remember or spell. It should tell in 1-3 words what you are about. Don't choose a name that is a disconnect from your business. You want clients to find you. Watch this video to get you thinking! (https://daretobeabadass.com/how-to-name-your-business-the-dos-and-donts/)

Branding Your Business — Your name will be your calling card but there are specific steps to make you recognizable to clients. Watch the video on Branding your business here. (https://daretobeabadass.com/branding-your-business/)

Build Your Bio — People want to know who they are doing business with. Writing out your bio will help them (and you) know what you are all about. Watch this video for bio building steps. (https://daretobeabadass.com/build-a-bio/)

The Pitch — Imagine you are on an elevator…you have three floors to tell them what you do for a living. What do you say that won't leave them running to the next exit? You want to leave them asking for more info. This video will help drive clients to you instead of scratching their heads. Watch here. (https://daretobeabadass.com/the-business-pitch/)

Build Your Business from Concepts to Profits — Got a great idea for a business? Start here with understanding the difference between a business verses a hobby. Then learn to monetize it! This 34-minute video will help you move your dreams forward. Watch Here. (https://daretobeabadass.com/build-your-business-from-concepts-to-profits/)

Business Check Off List — Starting a business is a daunting task with so much to remember. Some things need to be done in a specific order and others can be completed simultaneously. Here's your check off list. (https://daretobeabadass.com/build-your-business-check-off-list/)

Organizing Your Home-based Business

(https://homeschoolbasicsa-z.com/build-a-home-based-business/getting-organized-build-your-own-opportunities/)

Staying organized is vital to a home-based business where typically you wear all the department head responsibilities. Multi-tasking is essential for the work at home business owner, and if you are not organized, tasks take several times longer than necessary. Truth is lack of organization can cause burn out, delays for clients, loss of customers, and even close a company. In a small business, time is a coveted commodity.

These tips may help you stay on top of your business and avoid working more hours for yourself than you would if you worked for someone else.

Start with Meditation

Before the day starts, take ten to fifteen minutes to determine what the greatest priority of the day will be (see the previous Lesson). Doing this will get you started on the right project and help to avoid wasting the day by being side-tracked.

Schedule Yourself

(https://homeschoolbasicsa-z.com/14-rules-for-keeping-the-life-work-balance/)

Know your weekly and monthly schedule. Keep an annual planner and mark when major projects need to be started and are due. Then focus what needs to be done monthly and on a weekly schedule. Keep a list of things that need to be done when they come up but keep moving on the tasks at hand. Then at the end of the day make a 'to do' list for the next day or schedule the item on a calendar. Keep a daily journal of jobs, contacts, phone numbers and items completed. Be as detailed as you can be. Write the date at the top of the page and always start a new page each day. You're building a business history and helping your memory by keeping all this information in one place. Trust me, a journal can save you more times than not.

Tax Information

This is one of the tasks that often gets lost in the process. If you are not a detail and/or OCD, place a wall file holder near your work area, label it receipts and drop every purchase, receipt, donation and working bills in it to sort later. Later one of the jobs you can farm out will be organizing these receipts into categories for the CPA at tax time.

Contacts and Clients

Often casual contacts convert to clients. If you lose their information, you have lost potential income. Or a contact might be an excellent networking individual for your business. When someone I have met gives me a business card, as soon as I'm able (not in front of them) I write down what we talked about, how they can help me or how I can help them and any other memorable info. If the contact is getting married or going through something tough, write it down and ask them about it next time you talk. Remember, people want to work with people who demonstrate that they care. Likewise, if you meet someone you feel will not be a good fit for your business, when you're out of eyeshot, throw the card away so you won't get bogged down with unnecessary paperwork.

Mind Your Business

Know who you are and what your business is about. If you make LED lights for gardens, do not get sidetracked by selling yogurt. FOMO (Fear of Missing Out) can take you and your business so off track that your energy can be too diversified. There are millions of opportunities available to business owners today; everyone has a webinar, podcast, training tools, conferences, and free downloads. Find the one thing that you do well; the one thing that you are passionate about and stick with it. Be a master of one service rather than a one-stop window shopping place.

Do what only you can do

There is an appropriate time to do every job in your business, but there is equally a time to hire help to do the time-consuming menial tasks. For example, a dentist makes more money by doing dental work rather than billing, setting appointments, and opening mail. Use programs like Fiverr or Online Assistant to do some of those tasks. I use single moms, college students and those that I know would appreciate a few extra dollars and have some time on their hands. I also use programs like Fiverr to do jobs for me that might take me hours to learn the program. For example, I spent 20+ hours attempting to place a slider in the header of my website. Realizing I was losing money by the hour, I paid a college guy $10 to fix it which he completed in about ten minutes.

Plan Your Work and Work Your Plan

Draw out your business plan and future. Categorizing your priorities and the phases of the business. Then focus, focus, focus! If you need help getting organized than hire a professional organizer. Invest in your business but be wary of the multitude of potential money pitfalls.

Make your office task-efficient, have a work plan for the day, turn off distractions, and delegate jobs that take you away from the main tasks that move your business forward.

Lack of organization can bury any business. If you can visualize your success, write it down, organize the jobs, and delegate what does not require you to do, be disciplined to stay the course, your business will be a success. Do not let a lack of organization stifle your business' growth. Committing a few moments daily focused on organizing your workspace and planning your attack will produce less frustration, shorter work hours and increased growth and profits. You got this!

10 ways to build your entrepreneur longevity career

Building a business can be A) invigorating, B) Frustrating, C) Exhilarating D) Exhausting, E) All of the above. Here are ten tried and tested tips to building longevity into your entrepreneur career:

1. **Take yourself on as a client first**. If you were coaching yourself into success, ask yourself what you really want to do. You need to know what you could get up every day and do even if there never was a paycheck. Your goal is to create financially freedom, but there may be long days ahead before your business is lucrative so being passionate about what you do can carry you through those times. Know why you are doing what you're doing.

2. **Set goals**. Realistic, smart goals. SMART goals are Specific, Measurable, Attainable, Relevant and Time-sensitive. A goal such as I want to lose weight is not a S.M.A.R.T. goal. If you say you want to lose 10 pounds in 30 days that takes the goal from a dream into a workable plan. Take time to plan well, then work the plan.

3. **Learn to say "Yes" to new experiences and opportunities**. If it is not illegal, fatal, or too far off your goals, try it. Experiences often teach you more about yourself than education, books, and psychoanalyzing. Sometimes a new experience can point your career in a direction you never thought about, and sometimes experiences may demonstrate that is not the direction you want to go in. Both are equally valuable.

4. **Listen more than you talk**. Ask people what they do, what made them go that direction, what their greatest regret and proudest moments are and what advice they would pass along. People want to talk about their success and pass on golden nuggets and trade secrets. Let them.

5. **Criticism and Cheerleading**. Understand that both criticism and cheerleading serve valuable purposes. Do not be afraid to ask how you're doing. Realize criticism is about your work, not about you. Listen to others' assessments, and praise, but also understand that there is a time to agree with them and make a change and there is a time to thank them politely and let the information fall on deaf ears.

6. **Keep several people around you for growth**: 1) one that is much further along in the game than you are and emulate what you can, 2) those that love everything you do, there purpose is not to grow you but are valuable for helping you to lick your wounds, 3) peers are a great place to talk shop, commiserate together, and build up your confidence, 4) associate with people who are nothing like you. They are an excellent source of new ideas, shining a light into yourself that you did not know existed, and appreciating views of life and business different from your own. Choose these people wisely. You won't want a group of negative Nellie's or lazy victims. Choose and be the person that inspires synergy.

7. **Owning your world**. Remember everything you do, develop, or become has the potential to influence others to rise to a higher level in their life. Set

a mission statement about who you are as a person and business. Then filter opportunities that align with that directive. Build a strong ethical filter and modify but do not deviate from your purpose. Remember, if you are everything to everyone, you really will not be your best for anyone.

8. **Character and Reputation**. You only get one. Good and bad reputations live for an exceptionally long time in people's minds. It's not impossible to rebuild or remake who you are, but once you've tarnished your character, it's a long hard climb to repairing it. On the flip side, other people want to align themselves with quality character and positive status. Do not apologize for who you are but ask yourself if you would want to align yourself with you if you were building a quality-controlled industry.

9. **Be Passionate**. One of the greatest gifts of being an entrepreneur is the freedom to be passionate about what you do. Getting up every day loving what you do will make the long hours and hard work worth it. Starting a business is much like pushing a large boulder up a steep hill. It is hard, but worth it. If it were easy, everyone would be doing it, so plow on.

10. **Stress and Fear**. There are several kinds of stress. Deadlines can be stressful, or they can be forced time management. Financial strain can sometimes be the motivation for ingenuity—use it. Failure can help you understand what's not working and inspire you to develop another plan. Do not let fear paralyze you. When fear stays bound up inside in an emotional state it can be crippling. Call it out, categorize it and then solve it or design a new plan.

11. **The balancing act**. Plan for success. Work hard at it. But do not live to work. As hard as it is, build working hours and stick to them. Appreciate those who work for you and value their 'off hours' time as well. Spend time with friends and family. Do not buy them off, spend time with them. If tomorrow everything you have hoped for in your entrepreneur dream explodes, it will be your family and friends that will be your saving grace, and supporters. Treat them well. Learn to spend time alone. Discover the value of just being still—no electronics, no agenda. Take ten minutes every day to breath, to clear your mental clutter and to listen quietly. It is harder than it sounds, but you'll be better for it.

Cleaning and De-cluttering

"When all else fails, cleaning house is the
perfect antidote to most of life's ills."
~ Sue Grafton

You can tell the state of a woman's mind by what the inside of her purse looks like. If my purse is a disaster, typically my life is chaotic. When my life is in order, seems my purse is too. Check your purse. How are you doing?

Why worry about cleaning your house? Besides the obvious bacteria fighting, virus killing reasons, cleaning and decluttering brings about an emotional order and calm. Simplifying leaves your brain free to be creative, efficient, and much more able to focus on the things that really matter in life. The adage "less is more" is never truer when seeking serenity and order. We underestimate the power of tranquility within our homes and relationships. Isn't it time we all learn to let go of things that do not matter, waste our lives, make us uncomfortable and steal time from true relationships?

If cleaning eliminates germs, boosting the immune system, how much more will our psych benefit from the same type of order?

Our closets are often another indicator of internal order or the lack of it. When I can pull out a blouse that still has purchase tags on it, then I am not present in my life. Retail therapy is a real 'thing' and indicates that we are in the 'fill the hole in my life' state rather than understanding our true needs.

Overbuying is costly, adding to financial burdens, and the clutter of a closet that is too full. When I was challenged to go through my closet and only keep what fit, and that made me feel like a million bucks wearing it, I was surprised at how few pieces I left hanging. Then something amazing happened… there was a visual calmness, and ease at getting dressed in the morning, simplified work doing laundry and I knew what my next purchases should be.

Who would have thought a simple act of cleaning my closet could give me the emotional return to the level it did?

Why declutter and clean?

Clutter cost money. Buying items twice because you cannot find the item even though you know you have it is expensive. Misplaced bills can cost money by missing due dates and paying late fees—and affects credit scores.

Clutter cost time. Not know where things are forces you to waste time looking for them when you could be completing the task. A ten-minute job might take 30-60 minutes by the time you find the tool you need to complete the task. This might mean the jobs look too big for a short time frame, which leads to not starting at all. Soon all those incomplete jobs may be the source of feeling overwhelmed.

Clutter crowds the brain. Ever notice how noisy a room that is filled to the brim can be on your brain? There is a quietness in your soul when the room around you is ordered and simplified. Experiences over things is a motto that can enhance your life.

Pick Up Your Sword:

1. Start with the drawers in your bathroom. Dump the contents out and only put back what you will use.

2. Move to the towel closet. Take everything out. Keep what you will use and donate or throw away the rest. Get rid of expired products. Now put things back in an eye appealing manner.

3. If it needs scrubbing, scrub. If it needs painting, paint.

4. Step back and enjoy.

Take this method to a bedroom. If you are not ready, start next on a hall closet, then move to a room that you can do in a short amount of time. Remember, don't do the entire room—pick a drawer, cabinet, closet and build from there.

If you work at small projects daily, in 30 days you will have the entire house completed. You will be amazed at the calm this decluttering will bring. When we first started this process, I had an entire back bedroom (supposedly the guest bedroom but you could not find the bed) filled with scrapbooking stuff.

When we talked to the family, I was surprised to find that NO ONE ever looked at the scrapbooks. So instead, we invest in two large digital frames and a picture scanner. I scanned all the photos that were special to us and put them onto the digital frames. Now when we gather as a family, not only do we see them but the stories surrounding them are discussed and laughter fills our table! And we have a guest room now!

I went through all the sheets in the house, put them in a pile. Then picked out two sets for every bed, placing a top sheet, bottom sheet, and pillowcases, in a matching pillowcase and put them in the appropriate room. All the remaining odd sheets were donated.

I was shocked at how many odd pots, pans, mixing bowls, etc. that I have accumulated as well. I took them all out, decided what I really used, and donated the rest. I bought a set of mixing bowls with lids that nestled into one another. Once I finished decluttering, I could have those gorgeous kitchen cabinets with glass doors or even open shelving. And the calm inspired me to try new recipes.

Try decluttering. It feels powerful to know what is in your pantry and what is not. There are so many places to gain advice for decluttering on the internet. Find your favorites and dig in! Here is one of mine: Becoming Minimalist (https://www. becomingminimalist.com/) by Joshua Becker

Charlotte Ray, (1850-1911),

https://www.blackpast.org/african-american-history/ray-charlotte-e-1850-1911/

the first African American lawyer and the first woman admitted to the bar. Well educated, she received her law degree from Howard University after disguising her gender as C.E.Ray. A teacher in New York City, she faced great hardships with race and gender to attain her goals. She was a strong advocate for woman's suffrage.

Clutter cleaning 911

"The object of cleaning is not just to clean,
but to feel happiness living within that environment."
~Maria Kondo

General De-cluttering Tips!

Sort mail at the post office ...

...if you can, only bring home what you need to deal with or pay. If you don't have a post office, open the mail near a garbage can and get rid of everything that doesn't need your attention. Open and pay bills immediately, or stack to pay as soon as you can. If you have one or two days a month designated to paying bills, you will not feel like it consumes your time daily. I used to feel like, I cannot pay them until I have the money, so I paid them the night before my paycheck arrived. I solved two problems this way. I handled money concerns two times a month and was forced to stay on budget by paying them just before my paycheck arrived. Prior to developing this plan, I would deposit or cash my check, and money seemed to slip through my fingers before I got all the bills paid. Then I stressed about how to get them paid for the rest of the month. Lack of working a plan cost me more than money, it cost me stress.

Kitchen drawers.

We all have them, that junk drawer for miscellaneous items that has now become several junk drawers full of items we might use one time a year. I finally decided to put everything from the drawers in the middle of the kitchen island and if I used it within a month, I put it back in a drawer. At the end of the month, everything I did not use (except the turkey baster) was put in a donation box. I left the box sitting in the garage for another month to see if I might go looking for something and take it out. Guess what? I didn't. After six months of living with the items in the drawers that were spared the donation box, I only repurchased one item—a zester. Now I'm careful to buy products that serve at least a dual purpose which keeps the drawers clutter free. I like the clutter less drawers so well, I find other ways to do the job of another 'tool' just to keep the drawers so they open and close without resistance.

Kitchen pans and lids.

See above! I repeated the same process with my pots and pan and their lids. I discovered, I'd accumulated far more cookware than I'll ever use and filled the donation box with the excess. Now I can stack and retrieve pans without the one I want being buried in the back of the cabinet. I remember one day thinking I need a bigger kitchen, when truth was, I needed less stuff!

Bathroom medicine cabinets.

Stop laughing, you know you have the same problem I had! Yes, I found unused medicine from 2005! I discovered four unused tubes of toothpaste. Maybe I bought them on sale, or I thought we might be out because I could not find it, but by the time we could get to the fourth tube of toothpaste it would be expired. I know you are checking; yes, toothpaste does expire! Start small. Go through one shelf in the bathroom cabinet, or the medicine cabinet or one drawer every day. This way the task will not be overwhelming, won't take more than ten minutes and in a week, you'll have a bathroom organized.

Ten Minutes.

Speaking of cleaning shelves or drawers, here is a technique that works for me. Dump everything in the drawer or on the shelf on your bed or a table. EVERYTHING! Then only put back what you know for certain you will use. You have ten minutes. Make quick decisions. Your subconscious knows better than your 'maybe I'll need that one day' brain. At the end of ten minutes anything that did not make it into the drawer or back on the shelf, donate or throw away. Then get it out of your house so you are not tempted to bring it back in.

Never step over...

...something that should be picked up. Build your life so that everything has a place. When it is out of place, either put it away or yell at someone to do so. If it does not make it in ten minutes, donate! If you have a family, let them all know this rule is in effect. Or better yet, place the item in a box that cannot be touched until they complete a chore of your choosing. Make the chore count: clean the cat box, vacuum, dishes, something that takes you time. You will either get more work done by others, or they will begin to start picking things up. Remember, you will be caught by your own rule, so play along with it so that they see you are not immune to the rule either.

No more later.

If you cannot do it right now, most likely you will not do it later. Eliminate it or do it now. If you are tired of saying I will do that later, then stop bringing things into your life that you do not have time for.

No wasted trips.

If you are moving from one end of the house to the other, always bring something with you that must go to that end. If I am going from my office to the other end of the house to use the master bathroom, I bring the clothes in the dryer with me (because I pass the laundry room) and when I return, I bring a basket of clothes that can be thrown in the washing machine when I return. No wasted trips.

Door Basket.

Keep a basket by the door you use most often when you leave the house. Drop in it things that must be returned, purchased, deposited, or taken with you the next time out of the house. I'll put in our basket library books, shopping list (except now I use Alexa), my workout clothes, my flipflops for my pedicure, my coupons, recycling, a non-perishable snack, and a bottle of water (so I don't spend money on water and food while running errands). This basket has saved me so many times, I cannot tell you. I hated getting to the store to buy groceries and the money saving coupons were sitting on my desk. Or my day took more time than I thought, I pull stop at fast-food drive through and sabotage my own healthy diet. It is simple to grab the basket and throw it in the car. Then at the end of the day, I have accomplished my tasks, saved money, and can cross off my to do list with pleasure because nothing was forgotten.

To Do Lists.

I have a to do list for the entire week—Monday -Friday. That's my week. I plan to be done and relax over the weekend, but to do that, I need to have the 'have tos' done. This 5-day paper mousepad planner by Knock Knock Stuff stays on my desk at all times. I can place things to do on days that it is either due, or where it fits in my schedule. Monday morning, I know exactly what I am doing day by day. I highly recommend this simple little list.

Plan Your Attack.

Use a planner to place important events and goals over a 12-month period. Some events stay the same: birthdays, anniversaries, conferences, work schedules, church, kids' activities, etc. Once these are marked on the planner, then the random events can be placed on the schedule. I keep one day a week to make phone calls, mentor, bake, grocery shop, run errands, give back to the community and extended family. That day is typically packed full from early until late but I know that in advance and plan for it. This allows me to have solid at homework days where I do not leave the house and can take care of my @Home Business, chores, gardening, and read a magazine!

Set Boundaries.

I have a 9-9 rule. No working, phone calls, managing crisis before 9 a.m., and after 9 p.m. My family and friends know this, my employees know this, and once you get to know me, I am not available unless it's bleeding or on fire before or after 9. It helps me focus during the day, and allows me to get my quiet times, exercise, and hubby time in before the day starts. This rule also allows shift down time before bedtime. I do not do chores, work, electronics (except DVR'd TV) after 9 pm. This rule keeps me sane and protects our family life and my sleep.

Schedule Fun.

We practice "work to live not live to work" but to do that we write on the calendar coffee times with friends, date nights, family dinners, and movie nights. We have a fire-pit we use often in the warmer months and are thrilled that our grown children show up to sit around the fire and talk story! Learn to say 'No' to opportunities that push in on these special times. I hate funerals when people say the nicest things about the person that is just graduated to heaven. We believe our Ohana members would be better served saying those pleasant things while they are still alive, so we plan for those times.

Remove Excess.

We live in a world of plenty. We are often drowning in possessions.

Decluttering brings a calmness. Perhaps it is something less to think about, but it quiets the visual stimuli. In a world today, where we are fueled by visual stimulation and often cued with tones, beeps, and auditory motivations, eliminating things that via for our attention can inspire serenity among the chaos.

You do not have to do everything, but try one thing, get good at it, and then adopt the next! Here is to your tranquility!

Pick Up Your Sword:

1. Are you ready to start the big projects? Go through your file cabinets and important papers. You can probably throw half of the papers away. Cleanse all the old papers you do not need, instruction manuals (you can find them all on the internet), and scan receipts (another great reason to get that scanner). This is a big project, so plan a reward when it is done (there is a reason we're doing this.) I set an appointment for a pedicure when I finished condensing 5 (4 drawer) file cabinets to 1!! I really had accumulated far more than I needed thinking that one day I might need it. I scanned as much into the computer to the cloud or Dropbox (in case the computer crashes) and was amazed at how little space I needed to run the household and two businesses.

2. Scan all the business cards you need into an app called CardKeeper. Then toss all the cards!

3. Dig into that clothes closet! This is another big project but one of the most rewarding.

Madam C.J.Walker, (1867-1919),

https://www.womenshistory.org/education-resources/biographies/madam-cj-walker

one of the first self-made African American, female millionaires. She's famous for creating hair-care products for black women. She sold them door to door and soon created a brand recognized throughout the country. She provided jobs for 40,000 people. She was also known for covering tuition for African American students and worked hard in the anti-lynching movement.

Finishing Strong or If I should die look here.

It takes as much energy to wish as it does to plan.
~Eleanor Roosevelt

The sandwich age is tough. That is the age between supporting young adults and caring for elderly parents. It also means that some of them are graduating to heaven. As the executor of several estates, we learned firsthand the overwhelming job of sorting through a loved one's paperwork, household properties and personal belongings. After our fourth family member's passing, we refused to do the same to our children who would be the executors of our estate.

I created a box holding all our essential paperwork and labeled it, "If Mom should die, look in here!" Below I have listed the items that a person stepping in for you after your passing should need. Be careful not to think that you are too young to do this. Think about who will step in after you if a freak accident or illness should occur. Who will take care of your children, your pets, your finances? Being prepared makes your transition easier for the people left behind.

Money does not grow on trees but it sure would be easier if the receipts would! Keeping track of receipts, files and important papers can mean the difference of wasting money or saving dollars. I used to put my important papers on a pile off to the side of my desk. Between knocking it over and the cat stretching out on them, my organization left little to be desired. I now use a couple of tricks to keep me organized.

First, I have a plastic file box that sits opened on a shelf in my office. Inside it, I keep:

- Insurance papers
- Home
- Business
- Life
- Health
    - Vaccines
    - Surgeries
    - Medications

- Pets
  - Health & license records
  - Emergency permission to treat.
  - Instructions for care of pets if you should die.
  - Dental
  - Car
  - Long term care
  - Prepaid burial policy
- Car titles/extra keys/maintenance records
- End of life choices/DNR's
- Certificates & Policy booklets
  - Marriage License
  - Social Security Papers
  - Birth certificates
- Taxes
  - Last seven years each with annual receipts
- Thick files for receipts
  - Personal
  - Business
- Loans
  - Mortgage
  - Credit card papers (take copies of front and back and record pins)
  - Car loans
  - Student loans
  - Personal loans
- Bank Accounts
  - Personal accounts
    - Checking
    - Saving
    - Investments

- Business accounts
  - Checking
  - Saving
  - Investments
- Investments
  - 401K's
  - IRA's
  - Annuities
- Misc. Accounts
  - Identity thief
  - Donation receipts
- Online Passwords
  - Keep a notebook with all your contact info, log in names, passwords, security Q&A

After I have labeled in colorful folders all these topics, then I place the documents inside. Then I also have a 3-slot wall hanging holder. It is divided up into Personal, Business and Misc. Every receipt I receive I place in one of the slots to be organized later. I have used this system for 10 years and it works for me—because I use it!

Go over your billing statements monthly. You would be surprised how many mistakes you might catch from overbillings. I once went on a vacation with the money I caught on a bill that had gone overlooked for 10 years.

Invest in a sturdy shredder and shred all personal information to avoid having your information compromised.

But then you need to go one step further. Involve a professional CPA. (http://daisybooks.net/) Their knowledge of informational needs will save you not only time but potentially tons of money.

Then I have a small box (the kind that look like books) for each person in our family. When I think of a special memory, picture, trinket, etc. I place it in their box. My executor knows to hand these boxes out following my death. My prayers are that they will bring warmth and a hug to those I leave behind.

<u>Ruby Bridges</u>, **(1954-present)**,

https://www.womenshistory.org/education-resources/biographies/ruby-bridges

was the first Black child to integrate an all white elementary school. In 1960, she was escorted by four federal marshals on her first day of school through a crowd of angry white parents. Her courage to change history began at the age of six! She created the Ruby Bridges Foundation to promote tolerance and create change through education.

"Don't follow the path. Go where there is not path and begin with a trail. When you start a new trail equipped with courage, strength and conviction, the only thing that can stop you is you!" ~ Ruby Bridges

Managing your time or Counting your minutes

"It's not enough to be busy...
the question is what are we busy about?"
~Henry David Thoreau

Too often we get comfortable in our lives until the day we wake up and wonder if this is all there is. As women we move in and out of phases and seasons at breakneck speed. Sometimes we need a mentor to point out what is coming. Mentoring each other helps us avoid the pitfalls made before. You know the saying, "Listen to your elders, you won't live long enough to make all the mistakes yourself" is never truer than when today's woman is multi-tasking with our hair on fire.

Did you wake up this morning and wonder, "Is this it?" Some days feel like a roller coaster racing down a spiral with no exit point. If you are like me, I planned my life as a wife, mother, entrepreneur, gardener, and community citizen...but somewhere it all got out of control. I found myself doing the day-to-day details which are essential to life and managing a family, but lacking cheerfulness. Joy was escaping me, and I did not know why.

Many women today find themselves in a marathon sprint from the moment their feet hit the floor until long after everyone has gone to bed. Gone are the days where the only job we have is to cook, clean and raise babies. We have added to the list of daily duties such as: school volunteering, sporting events (that use to be a one-to-two-day commitment but now involves 6 days a week), church activities, and _____ you fill in the blank.

Most households today require two incomes to survive, otherwise one spouse carries all the income weight and misses out on co-parenting. And many of us are single parents struggling to be two parents.

Most of us attempt the American Dream and live beyond our means. With that said, most of us will need to either raise our income or lower our outgoing expenses. However, if you are not brand new to the game, you'll need to raise income to lower the expenses for a time. What if you are a single parent, or just single? How do you survive the insurmountable cost of just living? We no longer are a society that works to live, we have become the slaves of living to work.

More than income, and finances, let us talk about the stress factor in today's world. Stress is the number one cause of many of the deadly diseases we face in our society. Our philosophy of "If I work harder, longer, faster, I'll get ahead" is dangerous. Unfortunately, the only place we will be first with that attitude is the morgue.

Stress is paramount to relationship destruction. When we need to plan our day by the minutes, we are anything but calm and responsive. At breakneck speed, we lack clarity, artistry, transparency, and precision. We eat too fast, make poor choices because the choices are in a fast-food drive through, we skip essential rest and workouts. We all know the facts regarding longevity, mobility, heart protecting movement, foods, and sleep, but we often ignore them until there is a crisis that forces us to reconsider our life. I am suggesting if we can do it when it's a matter of life and death, why not do it before we've painted ourselves into a corner or checked into the emergency room?

Our current lifestyles may teach us new words to google, such as: anxiety, diabetes, high blood pressure, stroke, impotence, COPD, PTSD, fertility issues, weight gain, Alzheimer's, depression, ulcerative colitis, ATF, sleep disorders, chronic fatigue, _____<--again, you fill in the blank.

Today's distractions can keep us spun out of whack and running on a rodent wheel getting nowhere. When we used to talk, or sit quietly with our thoughts, fish, play, have tea, cuddle, or a wide variety of soul filling activities, we now fill our time with distractions. Most homes have a TV in every room, several computers, cell phones, iPad, Laptops, Facebook, twitter, TikTok, or ten other new things that will come out before I put the last period on this page.

We cannot think when our lives are run at the speed of sound. Our children grow from Pampers to anxiety meds with only a stop in the middle to be called ADD or ADHD.

Let's talk about purpose. That 'thing' that makes getting up in the morning worthwhile. Besides the people in our lives that we love, life should be lived giving and bringing purpose to others. When we are purposeless, we do not just invite depression, affairs, addictions, disconnect, debt, and disease into our lives, we fling the door wide open and enthusiastically welcome the monsters in.

Am I saying slow down? YES! But with a plan.

Ten minutes a day will create intentional living for the life you want to live.

This ultimate guide to living on purpose does not have a magic formula to copy and paste into your life. What it does have is a plan. Everyone has the same 24 hours a day to use or lose. When you subtract eight hours for sleep (I know you're not sleeping that much, but you should be so let's plan for it), eight hours for work (let's learn how to build a passive income so you can cut your hours down), two hours a day for eating (planning and preparing 3 meals a day), 2 hours of preparation (showering, dressing, etc.) and commute time, 1 hour of Facebook, cell and email time (I know I'm WAY underestimating this) and 1.5 hours of daily chores essential for surviving (shopping, laundry, dishes, animals, etc.) and 30 minutes to workout, walk, garden or breath. That leaves 60 minutes every day to build your dream.

Sixty minutes at your present life speed may sound like a lot of time to give up for this plan. But if we can use the first ten minutes of the day to plan the day, that leaves fifty minutes to dream a dream. The trick is in the planning and learning to eat an elephant one bite at a time.

Fifty minutes does not seem like a lot of time to build an entire dream. And it is not, but if you plan the time wisely, and consistently honor the time, you'll be amazed at the things you can accomplish. This is my eating an elephant one spoonful at a time theory. No one can possibly eat an entire elephant in one sitting. Most people will fail to start because the task looks too massive. However, if every day (supposing you could keep an elephant fresh) you ate a spoonful, within a short about of time, you would finish the task or at the very least make a large dent in it. If you show up daily, with the task in mind, you will soon satisfy the dream.

What's your dream? Is it to build your income, lose weight, organize your house, learn a foreign language, or build a house? Perhaps you have more than one dream, that's ok, this plan will still move you toward success.

List your dreams:

1. _____

2. _____

3. _____

4. _____

5. _____

Perhaps today is the first time in an awfully long time that you've even asked yourself, what your dream is. Let yourself be still. Alone with your thoughts, ask yourself, "What do I want?"

Remember dreams often change as we mature, environments change, life cycles change, etc. Take the time today to ask what you want. If you do not want anything more in your life, then today you've framed your own happiness and maybe all you needed was to realize it.

For some of us, asking the question and coming up with an answer might be the hardest part of this journey. It's easy to complain, to blame shift our happiness, or to simply stay on the merry-go-round without time to ask.

A year ago, someone challenged me to simply sit still, away from all distractions, alone with my thoughts for ten minutes a day. They gave me a journal that I was to fill out following the ten minutes. Being an A-type personality, I poo pooed the idea and figured it would be a cinch. It wasn't.

Quieting my mind from the day's activities was tough. Giving myself permission to sit still was tough. Pushing myself to have something to write in the journal was frustrating. Until one day I simply gave up. I sat on a bench by our koi pond. I did nothing. I looked around. I breathed. I noticed things around me. I cleared my mind.

I gained clarity, felt centered, refreshed, and relaxed. I wrote down my day's priorities. I wrote down my goals. I even wrote down my strengths and decided where I was off track from using them. Because I had made a list of A,B and C priorities, I attacked the A items and got twice as much done in half the time.

A,B and C priorities are: A=things that must be completed today. B=things that need to get done this week. C=things I need to do when I can. The upside is going to bed relaxed with all the A items and maybe a little B job completed. I felt satisfied that I had been productive. And it brought at sense of calm. I also gave me a sense of 'not everything has to be done today' and I would audibly say, "That's a Monday job, or that's a Friday job."

The following day, pad in hand, I spent my ten minutes moving B items to A's, etc. I even had more time to do what I wanted to do because I had completed the A items. Suddenly, jobs that used to take an hour to complete, I was getting done in 15 minutes and freeing up parts of my day.

Another thing that helped me be productive was a knee injury. Yes, I said a knee injury. Because I did not opt for the surgery, I had to commit to following the physical therapist's directions exactly. One of those instructions was to never sit more than 60 minutes. As a freelance writer, my job is completed sitting. At the end of 60 minutes, I had to change activities. I would do the laundry, dishes, walk the dogs, vacuum, and fill the wood box. After moving, I could go back to my chair for another 60 minutes.

I had to set the clock on my phone to remind me to get up. The thing that amazed me most was that I now was extremely aware of the clock ticking and dug into my work, completing more things than I had in the past. I'm using it right now to clear my article deadlines.

Here's the thing: 60 minutes is 60 minutes. We can waste them, or we can use them to our advantage. But for 60 minutes every day use them to bring you closer to your dreams.

For instance, if you want to lose weight, take 60 minutes a day to plan for your success. Start your day with 30 minutes of work out, and take a half hour to plan, shop, and make your food for the day. I like to make our dinner in the crock pot while I'm cooking my breakfast immediately following my workout. I also do the dishes while I'm cooking. And somehow because I've started the day with activity, planning my food, and a clean kitchen, the 'get it done' mentality seems to perpetuate a momentum for the entire day.

It takes some forethought and some organization to get you on the road to living your dream. But 60 minutes a day, does not rob from anyone, and it creates better time management for the rest of the day for your home, your family, and your friends.

I am a strong proponent of organizing my day on a calendar.

Once you see your life on paper, you can begin to eliminate wasteful time. Maybe your phone needs to go in a drawer to avoid distractions. I have two computers for my work. The desk computer is for sending off articles, social media, marketing, and research. On creative writing days, I work on a laptop that is not connected to the internet, Facebook, email, etc. I intentionally work away from my desk, and the distractions that can kill my 60 minutes. I also start with 'money making' projects first, then move to things like networking, emails, etc. But I also have a hard fast rule that my family calls, "No Crap before 9 a.m." I do not pay bills, make phone calls, answer texts, emails, and the like before 9 a.m. I need to protect the time before my husband goes to work, my workouts, my coffee sipping time, and my quiet times. I refuse to start my day at a sprint because it sets the tone for the rest of the day. If I'm not careful, I'll be back in that working longer, harder, faster mode we talked about earlier.

I have learned to compartmentalize my life into before work and after work hours. I do not work when it's family time, play time, chore time, meditation time and dinner time. But when it is work time, I work. I work in 60-minute cycles. Each cycle has its purpose. I do not do crossover purposes. For instance, I don't multitask my marketing time and my writing time. Those activities use vastly different parts of the brain. When I used to multi-task, I found I did several things half well, or at the least less than my best. The 60-minute purpose helps me to 1) define what will happen during the 60 minutes, 2) give me a time limit to attain the goal, 3) keep me from being stuck and move on to the next task. I keep a quote near my desk that reminds me to keep moving forward on my goals. It says:

"If you can't fly, then run,
If you can't run, then walk,
If you can't walk, then crawl,
But whatever you do,
You have to keep moving forward."
~ Martin Luther King

Pick Up Your Sword:

1. If you have answered the question, "What do I want," now you need to answer the question- "How will I get it?" Success can look quite different to every person. Look back on your "What do I want" choices, and number them in order of priority, then let's work with your number one choice.

   _____

   _____

   _____

   _____

2. How will I get it?

   _____

   _____

   _____

3. What is it today that is stopping you from getting what you want?

   _____

   _____

   _____

The bottom line? We all have the same 24-hour day. Ten minutes a day to set the day's priorities will create an opportunity to get more done and move closer to your real dreams—Your purpose. Isn't that what we all want? To live out a purposeful life regardless of what that purpose is.

Try it. Ten minutes to plan, 60 minutes set aside for your dream. Try it for a month, or a week. You will be surprised how much of that elephant you can eat in a short amount of time.

"Dreams stay dreams without planning and deadlines."
~Pam Vincent

Finding Your Purpose

"There are only two ways to live your life.
One is as though nothing is a miracle.
The other is as though everything is a miracle."
~ Albert Einstein

Finding our purpose in life is much like an onion; you peel it one layer at a time. Each time we peel a layer, another new level appears. Now that we have taken the time in past Lessons to define our giftings, energy levels, personality bents, learning styles and season in life, we can more clearly see what we are really passionate about. Next, we need to clarify who we will be serving with our talents. We may be called to use our talents in a far-off country, work with jr. higher, serve food to the homeless, run a corporation, care for the elderly or many other opportunities. The importance of all we have learned is that we do what only we can do or are called to do.

As a young person, it's common not to know our purpose. It is also just as vital that we try on many passions to understand the one that generates a fire within us. Do not discount the trials, pain, and failures; they are the ones that teach the deepest lessons and often show us our path. We cannot allow those 'negative' experiences to live our lives in safe mode. The good, bad, and tough events write a script for our 2nd and 3rd act.

Scripture reminds us we are God's masterpiece and created to do good things. A masterpiece is an artist's unique expression of something that moves deep inside of them. We are God's unique creation that brings Him joy. He has knit us together with skills, gifts, passions, and personalities that He delights in. We have been given a task here on earth. Our job is to discover it and pursue living a life that brings us, others, and our Lord delight.

Mark Twain said, "The two most important days in life are the day you were born and the day you find out why."

We've all experienced that feeling that says, "Something's not right." We feel out of place or like a square peg in a round hole. Sometimes we must walk along this path to get where we really want to be. We can fake it for a while, but our passion will either wane or we will just go through the motions of living, until our spirits become so restless, we think we will explode. There comes a moment where we know we are meant for more.

If we consistently pursue our purpose, our skills, our passion, our audience, and our joy will align. Our spirits soar, our misgivings quiet and it feels right. There is an overwhelming feeling that says, "This is where I am meant to be." There is no more time left for stumbling through life. We must actively seek to develop the service that lies within us.

"Don't live carelessly, unthinkingly.
Make sure you understand what the Master wants."
~Ephesians 5:17 (MSG)

What are you uniquely designed to do? What are the things you are passionate about and if money and time were no object what would you get up in the morning excited to do? What do you find yourself naturally doing that you do better than most people?

Like a track long jumper, the goal is always to land falling forward. Great things happen when we keep our purpose in mind and continue to strive toward it.

What's the secret to a purpose driven life?

Know God. Read your Bible daily. When you read something that tells you what you should be doing—do it!

Know you. Understand what you are equipped to do and stay in your lane. Don't imitate others unless you are certain that's who you can pattern yourself after.

Know your enemy. Don't underestimate who aims to take you down. Gird yourself with prayer. Surround yourself with like-minded people while you are engaged in the battle.

Build a circle of 5!

- Develop a prayer warrior,

- Find a mentor,

- Find a person with the gift of exhortation who can give you nuggets of truth,

- Find a person with the gift of wisdom and ask their advice,

- Find a mercy with the gift of mercy that you can lick your wounds with.

Run your race. Like Nike says, "Just do it!" Slaughter the nay-sayers in your head and start serving. No one is perfect or even really good at it when you first get started. You will gain clarity as you go, but God cannot direct a ship that's sitting still. Pick Up Your Sword and Start today!

Pick Up Your Sword:

1. *"For I am the Lord, your God, who takes hold of your right hand and says to you, do not fear; I will help you." ~ Isaiah 41:13*
    How will we know and serve our purpose according to Isaiah?

    _____

    _____

    _____

2. *"Commit to the Lord whatever you do, and your plans will succeed."*
    ~ Proverbs 16:3 (NIV)
    According to Proverbs will we be successful?

    _____

    _____

    _____

3. *"Have I not commanded you? Be strong and courageous. Do not be terrified; do not be discouraged, for the Lord your God will be with you wherever you go. ~ Joshua 1:9 (NIV)*
    Why should we move forward even when we are scared?

    _____

    _____

    _____

4. *"The Lord has established His throne in heaven, and his kingdom rules overall. Praise the Lord, you His angels, you mighty ones who do His bigging, who obey His word. Praise the Lord, all His heavenly host, you His servants who do His will. Praise the Lord, all His works everywhere in His dominion. Praise the Lord, my soul." ~ Psalms 103:19-22 (NIV)*
    Your thoughts:

    _____

    _____

    _____

5. *"His master replied, 'Well done my good and faithful servant! You have been faithful with a few things; I will put you in charge of many things."*
    ~ Matthew 25:21 (NIV)
    Is this what you want said to you the day you arrive in heaven? What's your mission statement?

    _____

    _____

    _____

6. "God made my life complete when I placed all the pieces before him. When I got my act together, he gave me a fresh start…God rewrote the text of my life when I opened the book of my heart to his eyes." ~ Psalm 18:20-24
What is the promise here?

_____

_____

_____

What might God be calling you to do?

_____

What is stopping you or stealing your purpose?

_____

Why?

_____

How will you squash the purpose stealer?

_____

When will you begin to live your purpose?
There is no line to write your answer because you begin today!

Pick up your Sword!
and
Dare to be a Badass!
Today!

Want to know Jesus?

If you do not know Jesus as your Savior, begin today. Below is how I asked Jesus into my heart and you can too!

1. **Man's Problem:** God loves you so much that he wants you to have an abundant life. We are sinful and that sin separates us from eternal life and knowing God intimately. Man's problem:

    a. *John 10:10 - "The thief comes only to steal and kill and destroy; I have come that they may have life and have it to the full." (NIV)*

    b. *Romans 3:23 - "for all have sinned and fall short of the glory of God," (NIV)*

    c. *Romans 6:23 - "For the wages of sin is death, but the gift of God is eternal life in Christ Jesus our Lord."*

2. **God's Solution:** He sent his son to die in place of our sins.

    a. *Romans 5:8 - "But God demonstrates his own love for us in this: While we were still sinners, Christ died for us."*

    b. *John 3:16 - "For God so loved the world that he gave his one and only Son, that whoever believes in him shall not perish but have eternal life." (NIV)*

    c. *1 Corinthians 15:3-6 - "For what I received I passed on to you as of first importance: that Christ died for our sins according to the Scriptures, 4 that he was buried, that he was raised on the third day according to the Scriptures, 5 and that he appeared to Cephas, and then to the Twelve. 6 After that, he appeared to more than five hundred of the brothers and sisters at the same time, most of whom are still living, though some have fallen asleep."*

    d. *John 14:6 - Jesus answered, "I am the way and the truth and the life. No one comes to the Father except through me.*

3. **Our Part:** We must each accept our sin, and God's provision for it by receiving Christ as our Savior.

    a. *John 1:12 - "Jesus answered, "I am the way and the truth and the life. No one comes to the Father except through me."*

b. Ephesians 2:8,9 - *"For it is by grace you have been saved, through faith—and this is not from yourselves, it is the gift of God— 9 not by works, so that no one can boast."*

c. John 3:1-8 - *"Now there was a Pharisee, a man named Nicodemus who was a member of the Jewish ruling council. ² He came to Jesus at night and said, "Rabbi, we know that you are a teacher who has come from God. For no one could perform the signs you are doing if God were not with him."*
³ Jesus replied, "Very truly I tell you, no one can see the kingdom of God unless they are born again."
⁴ "How can someone be born when they are old?" Nicodemus asked. "Surely they cannot enter a second time into their mother's womb to be born!"
⁵ Jesus answered, "Very truly I tell you, no one can enter the kingdom of God unless they are born of water and the Spirit. ⁶ Flesh gives birth to flesh, but the Spirit gives birth to spirit. ⁷ You should not be surprised at my saying, 'You must be born again.' ⁸ The wind blows wherever it pleases. You hear its sound, but you cannot tell where it comes from or where it is going. So it is with everyone born of the Spirit."

d. Revelations 3:20 - *"Here I am! I stand at the door and knock. If anyone hears my voice and opens the door, I will come in and eat with that person, and they with me."*

4. **God's Promise:** Once we have made that commitment, God's promise to us is that our sins have been washed clean, we receive the Holy Spirit within our hearts, and we are promised to spend eternity in Heaven with Him.

a. 1 John 5:11-12 - *And this is the testimony: God has given us eternal life, and this life is in his Son. 12 Whoever has the Son has life; whoever does not have the Son of God does not have life.*

b. John 14:21 - *Whoever has my commands and keeps them is the one who loves me. The one who loves me will be loved by my Father, and I too will love them and show myself to them.*

5. **Celebrate!** Assurance

a. Revelations 3:20 - *"Here I am! I stand at the door and knock. If anyone hears my voice and opens the door, I will come in and eat with that person, and they with me."*

b. Colossians 1:27 - *"To them God has chosen to make known among the Gentiles the glorious riches of this mystery, which is Christ in you, the hope of glory."*

c. *John 5:24* - *"Very truly I tell you, whoever hears my word and believes him who sent me has eternal life and will not be judged but has crossed over from death to life."*

d. *2 Corinthians 5:17* - *"Therefore, if anyone is in Christ, the new creation has come: The old has gone, the new is here!"*

e. *1 Thessalonians 5:18* - *"Give thanks in all circumstances; for this is God's will for you in Christ Jesus."*

Here's a simple prayer to invite Christ into your life: Dear God, I recognize that I'm a sinner and that sin keeps me from sharing eternity with you. I believe that you died on the cross and took all my sins upon yourself so I would not have to. Please forgive me and come into my heart to rule my life. I believe You have forgiven my sins; past, present and future, allowing me to be bound to you with the promise of heaven following my death. Thank you for coming into my heart and ruling my life. Amen.

If you just prayed this prayer for the first time—welcome to the kingdom!

Email me so I can celebrate with you! pjvincent@rconnects.com

How do you Grow in Christ?

Go to God in prayer daily (John 5:17)

Read God's word daily (Acts 17:11)

Obey God moment by moment (John 14:21)

Witness for Christ by your life and words (Matthew 4:19 and John 15:8)

Trust God for every detail of your life (1 Peter 5:7)

Holy Spirit – allow Him to control and empower your daily life and witness (Galatians 5:16,17 and Acts 1:8)

Read your Bible daily—even if only for a minute ßGod can use that commitment.

When you find a nugget that you know God expects of you, obey it and get it done. When He asks you to do hard things—do it! Enjoy the fellowship with others and find a prayer accountability partner.

Chapter 52

How to Demonstrate God's Love to Others

"Greater love hath no man than this,
that a man lay down his life for his friends.
Ye are my friends, if ye do whatsoever I command you."
~John 15:13-14

Sharing the greatest gift of life with another person is exciting, difficult, a blessing and terrifying. When we know the way to eternal life, we are compelled to share it. Our enemy has tainted people to such a degree that sharing our faith becomes a tightrope walk between being seen as a zealot or being too passive. Because we are leaders in the war against going to hell, we will find ourselves in contact with those that have been hurt by the church or a well-meaning Christian. People can be cruel to people and when it is a Christian that does the hurting, the pain cuts like a knife. Worldly influences can give a wide berth of reasons to not be interested in knowing Christ. Sharing our faith can be petrifying regardless of the thumping in our chest and our love for an individual…, but we need to try anyway.

There are statistics that tells us people come to accept Christ as their savior most often because someone asked them. We need to create the habit of asking or earning the rite to be close enough to the person to be able to ask.

Sometimes witnessing to others will be a simple question: Do you want to know Christ?

Sometimes witnessing will be another person's view of our lives that demonstrates our love for the Lord.

Sometimes witnessing will be standing in the gap with a person going through struggles/pain/loss.

Sometimes witnessing will be the quiet strength demonstrated day-to-day for years before a person is open to hearing about salvation.

Often times, more so than not, we must live our lives in such a way that God's love is demonstrated over and over for years. Then when a day comes that our 'friend' is confronted by life in a way that only God can comfort, we will have earned the rite to speak about His love and provisions for salvation.

Truth is we will all live forever, we must choose where that will be; heaven or hell.

I remember once years ago someone asking me, "If you are taken to court and prosecuted for being a Christian—will there be enough evidence to convict you?" That has stayed with me since.

Being a front runner, you will meet trials and struggles as you seek to obey the commandment to tell others about Christ. Never underestimate your role as an enemy to the enemy. Satan will use every opportunity to take you down and he is an expert at knowing your achilleas heel (weak spots.) You will need your armor to protect you, and you must be strong enough to pick up your sword!

Pick Up Your Sword:

1. *"I am the true vine, and my Father is the gardener. 2 He cuts off every branch in me that bears no fruit, while every branch that does bear fruit he prunes so that it will be even more fruitful." ~ John 15:1-2*
   What does this verse say about Christians not doing God's work?

   _____

   _____

   _____

2. *"I am the vine; you are the branches. If you remain in me and I in you, you will bear much fruit; apart from me you can do nothing. ⁶ If you do not remain in me, you are like a branch that is thrown away and withers; such branches are picked up, thrown into the fire and burned. ⁷ If you remain in me and my words remain in you, ask whatever you wish, and it will be done for you. ⁸ This is to my Father's glory, that you bear much fruit, showing yourselves to be my disciples." ~ John 15: 5-8*
   What are the promises to you as a worker for Christ?

   _____

   _____

   _____

3. *"My command is this: Love each other as I have loved you. ¹³ Greater love has no one than this: to lay down one's life for one's friends. ¹⁴ You are my friends if you do what I command." ~ John 15:12-14*
   What is our job?

   _____

   _____

   _____

4. *"If the world hates you, keep in mind that it hated me first. 19 If you belonged to the world, it would love you as its own. As it is, you do not belong to the world, but I have chosen you out of the world. That is why the world hates you." ~ John 15:18-19*
    Who do we belong to?

    _____

    _____

    _____

5. *"But this one thing I do, forgetting what is behind, and straining toward what is ahead, I press on toward the goal to win the prize for which God has called me ..." ~ Philippians 3:13-14*
    What are we encouraged to do when living our lives committed to Christ? (even when it's hard)

    _____

    _____

    _____

6. *"His master replied, 'Well done, good and faithful servant! You have been faithful with a few things' I will put you in charge of many things. Come and share your master's happiness!" ~ Matthew 25:23*
    This was said by a master to his servant for a job well done. This should be our goal standing face to face with Christ at the end of our life. What do you think a faithful servant looks like?

    _____

    _____

    _____

How to give your testimony (or tell your story of when you invited Christ into your heart)

Your story should be told in only a few minutes. No matter how exciting your salvation experience was, you only have 2-3 minutes to capture a person's interest. So you need to practice giving your testimony quickly and concisely without losing the heart of the story. Here are a few ideas to get you started:

1. What was your life like before you decided to you needed Christ in your life?

   _____

   _____

   _____

2. Why did you decide Jesus was the way for you?

   _____

   _____

   _____

3. Where were you and who were you with?

   _____

   _____

4. What has your life been like since you made this important decision?

   _____

   _____

   _____

Practice telling your story and time yourself. 3 minutes max.

Practice telling your story to another Christian. Ask them to evaluate it.

Commit to telling your story in a natural conversation with someone you know does not know Christ.

Once they've made the decision, help them pick up their sword and grow.

Thank you for purchasing Dare to be a Badass. I pray you were challenged and found some golden nuggets to use. You Rock! I pray you are brave enough to be different.

Let this be your Theme Song: Different by Micah Tyler

Other places to find Pam:

Dare to be a Badass https://daretobeabadass.com

Podcast:

https://anchor.fm/pamala-j-vincent

HomeSchool Basics A-Z   https://homeschoolbasicsa-z.com/

Facebook:

https://www.facebook.com/BadassWarriorWomen

https://www.facebook.com/pamalajvincent

https://www.facebook.com/GardensOpinion

Other books by Pamala J Vincent:

Lessons from the Garden Series:

- Seeds of Daily Inspiration
  (https://daretobeabadass.com/product/daily-seeds-of-wisdom/)

- For the Love of Pets
  (https://daretobeabadass.com/product/for-the-love-of-pets-2/)

- The Real Dirt on Being Happy
  (https://daretobeabadass.com/product/the-real-dirt-on-being-happy-2/)

- Seeds of Wisdom for Parents
  (https://daretobeabadass.com/product/seeds-of-wisdom-for-parents-and-grandparents-2/)

- Holi-dazes!
  (https://daretobeabadass.com/product/holidazes-2/)

Between a Rock and a Teenager Series:

- Between a Rock and a Teenager
  (https://homeschoolbasicsa-z.com/product/between-a-rock-and-a-teenager/)

- Getting the Job for Teens and Rookies
  (https://homeschoolbasicsa-z.com/product/getting-the-job-for-teens-and-rookies/)

- How to Get What You Want
  (https://homeschoolbasicsa-z.com/product/how-to-get-what-you-want/)

- Making the Grade
  (https://homeschoolbasicsa-z.com/product/making-the-grade/)

- Rookie Chefs on a Budget
  (https://homeschoolbasicsa-z.com/product/rookie-chefs-on-a-budget/)

- Teen Exit Strategy Techniques
  (https://homeschoolbasicsa-z.com/product/teen-exit-strategy-techniques/)

HomeSchool Basics A-Z Series: (Scope and Sequence)

- What to Teach Your Preschooler
  (https://homeschoolbasicsa-z.com/product/what-to-teach-your-preschooler/)

- What to Teach Your Kindergartener
  (https://homeschoolbasicsa-z.com/product/what-to-teach-your-kindergartener/)

- What to Teach Your 1st Grader
  (https://homeschoolbasicsa-z.com/product/what-to-teach-your-1st-grader/)

- What to Teach Your 2nd Grader
  (https://homeschoolbasicsa-z.com/product/what-to-teach-your-2nd-grader/)

- What to Teach Your 3rd Grader
  (https://homeschoolbasicsa-z.com/product/what-to-teach-your-3rd-grader/)

- What to Teach Your 4th Grader
  (https://homeschoolbasicsa-z.com/product/what-to-teach-your-4th-grader/)

- What to Teach Your 5th Grader
  (https://homeschoolbasicsa-z.com/product/what-to-teach-your-5th-grader/)

- What to Teach Your 6th Grader
  (https://homeschoolbasicsa-z.com/product/what-to-teach-your-6th-grader/)